Wife of the —
of the
Deceased

*A Memoir
of Love, Loss, and Learning to Live Again*

Dawn M. Bell

Ninety percent of net profits will be donated to established programs to combat child abuse, neglect, and sex trafficking. Primary focus will be on The Porch Light to rescue and restore child victims of sex trafficking and prevent the impact of sex slavery for future generations.

www.ThePorchLight.org

Disclaimer: The views and opinions expressed in this book are solely those of the author. The events related in this memoir, including conversations that occurred, have been re-created to the best recollection of the author. Some situations have been modified, compressed, or expanded; names and identifying details of certain individuals have been changed for confidentiality purposes.

Published by
Dawn M. Bell
Winter Park, FL

Printed in the United States of America

Library of Congress Control Number: 2014947478
Bell, Dawn M.

FIRST EDITION

ISBN: 978-0-9906438-1-4

Jacket art direction and graphic design by: Kymi Swanepoel
Front jacket photo: Microsoft PowerPoint 2010, Wedding Ring provided by Fotolia #56079667 Wedding Ring on White
© Melking

Printing and binding by A & A Printing, Inc., Tampa, FL

Back cover "ussie" photo by Matthew C. Bell, August 2010

For you, Matty.

Acknowledgments

A special thank you to my editor, Bobbie Christmas, at Zebra Communications. Not only did you edit my manuscript with exceptional skill, you confirmed the necessity for such a resource. This memoir may never have been published if not for your support and encouragement.

To my beta readers:
Susan Bennett, Teresa Bruce, and Katie Daniel.
Thank you for the selfless gift of your time.

1

Early November 2010

I looked down at my wrist. *It will be so easy to slice, switch hands, and cut the other side. I'll lie back, close my eyes, and fall asleep. It will be over, and I can see him again.*

Tears slid down my face.

How can he really be gone? How can I never see him again? How can I live without him? How did this happen?

Questions swirled in my mind like a spiteful tornado as my sobbing rose to a hysterical wail. My crying became so intense I squeezed out every last breath and then could not inhale, because my diaphragm locked up. I fell into a torturous cycle of bawling—suffocation—bawling—suffocation. Tears poured down my swollen face for hours.

I ran to the closet and wrenched his shirts from their hangers. I drew them to me, aching to touch what was left of him. I needed to smell him and forget he was gone if only for a few seconds. I needed to pretend he was with me.

I dropped to the floor and buried my face in his clothes. For a few seconds I could smell his scent, but it evaporated. Extensive crying caused my nasal membranes to swell closed, and I could breathe only through my mouth. I was denied the grain of comfort I sought.

How can my body be so cruel? How can it betray me? I give up. I give up. I. Give. Up. I cannot go on. I don't want to go on. I cannot lift myself from this floor. I have nothing to get up for. I have no one to get up for. Ava will be fine without me. She'll eventually understand. She'll do just as well without me. Let it end! God, please let it end. I beg you, please take me from this hell. I know you can do it if you choose to.

Those thoughts spun around and around in my head as I lay balled up on the closet floor clinging to Matt's clothes. I had hit rock bottom. I knew taking my own life would never be a real option; my resilience would not allow it. *But would I stop someone else?* I pictured a burglar standing over me with the intention of ending me. *Would I run? Would I put up a fight?*

No.

While I could not do it myself, I wouldn't have stopped someone else from freeing me of my agony and hopelessness. Not that day.

I fell asleep from total exhaustion and awoke some time later. My crusted eyes burned. I looked over the disaster of shirts I was still clutching in my arms as if through rigor mortis. I tried to comprehend the energy and effort it would take to crawl out of my deep hole. *Can I pick myself up and carry on?* I had to try.

2

Two Months Earlier

The morning of Friday, September 3, 2010, started in a scramble. I took the day off to make it a four-day holiday weekend and was in a rush to get myself dressed for a nine o'clock doctor's appointment. I prodded my four-year-old daughter to stay on track and get ready for pre-K, also at nine. If all went smoothly, I would drop her off and get to my appointment with three minutes to spare.

I darted into our home office to finish up a five-page expense report and fax it in to work. This process was always tricky, because my receipts had to be taped to blank pages and were known to get stuck in the fax machine causing a paper jam. I then had to start the process all over again, which never failed to test my patience, not something I had time for that morning.

Pages one and two went through, page three was in progress, and page four was on deck. *One last page, and I'm home free.* Ring! Someone called our home phone and kicked me off the fax machine. What? My whole body tensed in frustration, I rolled my eyes. *You've got to be kidding me!*

I snatched the phone and looked at the caller ID to see who just threw a wrench in my morning. It's Matt. My dear husband of fourteen years was calling me. *What is he thinking?* He knew this would be a crazy morning and I needed to be out the door early so I could drop off our daughter and get to my appointment on time. He never called in the morning; it was kind of a rule. I took a deep breath, forced a smile, and answered the phone.

"Hey, Matty! What's up?" I asked as cheerfully as I could.

"Hi, Dawn, not much, I've got a four-hour wait before we take off from Dubai. This city is amazing. How's your morning?"

"Good, I'm just running a bit behind to get Ava to school, and remember, I've got that doctor's appointment."

"Oh, that's right. Sorry, I won't keep you. I just wanted—"

"Hi, Daddy! It's Ava!" Our four-year-old daughter giggled, cutting him off. She apparently had picked up the living room extension.

Ugh! I silently grumbled as I watched the minutes tick away. I closed my eyes and pinched between them. I inhaled deeply to incite patience and listened to the sweet conversation between my husband and our daughter. They said good-bye, and Ava hung up.

"When did she learn to answer the phone?" Matt asked.

"That's only the second time she's done it. I taught her the other day. I think I've created a monster." I laugh.

"Thanks for all the pictures of Dubai. They're great. I can't wait to hear all about it, but hon, I've really got to get going. I'm sorry to cut you off."

"No problem, I just wanted to call and hear your voice. Oh, and I e-mailed you a great link on YouTube; you're going to love it. I'll call you tonight from Cologne. Olive juice."

"Olive juice more," I said and hung up the phone.

I smiled, knowing his way of saying "I love you" to avoid heckling when other guys were around. He'd done it since college because when you mouth the words 'I love you', it looks like you're saying olive juice.

I somehow made it out the door, dropped Ava off, and got to the doctor's office on time. I walked back out at 9:46. I texted Matt to tell him everything went okay at my appointment. I apologized again for cutting our earlier conversation short and told him I didn't deserve him.

His text response: Sweet!!!!!! I love y o u!

My text response: Ditto

3

Early Afternoon, September 3, 2010

I finished the morning errands and went home for lunch. I queued up the previous night's episode of *Project Runway*, ready to enjoy a favorite show. The phone rang, and the caller ID read UPS. I said "Hello" thinking someone in the Scheduling Department was calling for Matt to fly overtime, mistakenly dialing his home and not his cell number.

"Hello, may I ask whom I'm speaking with?" the caller asked.

"Dawn Bell," I responded. *You called me, right?*

"Are you related to Matthew Bell?" she asked. I chuckled to myself. *I certainly didn't marry someone I'm related to.*

"He's my husband. He just left Dubai. I can give you his cell phone number, if you're trying to reach him."

"So you know he's at work, and you say he's in Dubai. Do you know where he is supposed to land?" she asked.

I was getting annoyed. *Why is this person asking such weird questions? If she's calling from UPS, why doesn't she know the answers?*

I decided to go along with it, "Yeah, he either just left Dubai or is about to, and he'll be in Cologne, Germany, some time this evening." I was slightly impressed with the fact that I knew what country he was in that morning and what country he was en route to. Being married to a pilot with a continually changing route made it incredibly hard to remember which state, country, or even continent he was in at all times, and add in the time zone change? Forget it.

The rest of the conversation is blurred. I remember her introducing herself and saying there had been an incident with Matt's plane. She suggested that I keep the television off and told me she would update me with the latest reports. She called several times over the next few hours and asked about other family members in the house and in the area.

I was confused by her cryptic calls. She couldn't tell me anything concrete but wanted to know if someone would be able to pick up my daughter from pre-K for me. She told me she was sending local UPS administrative personnel to my house.

"Why?" I asked, but the most she would tell me was that there was an incident and the pilots may have been injured.

She suggested I call my brother who lives an hour from me in Florida, as well at the rest of my immediate family in the Midwest. She wanted me to give them a heads-up about the situation.

My irritation rose. "What situation?" I screamed at her. "You're not telling me anything, but you want me to call our families and worry them over nothing? I won't do that!" I couldn't believe anything bad had happened. If there was an incident, the company was overreacting and it was only that the plane slid off the runway or a bird flew into the engine as it was taxiing.

I called my friend Angelina, who was on her way to my house from Miami to spend Labor Day weekend with me. I told her what was going on and asked her what she thought it meant.

"I don't know," she said, "but I know if Matt can get home, he will do everything in his power to get to you and Ava."

Two UPS men I had never met came to my home. They waited until Angelina arrived to give me the unbelievable news. The cargo jet Matt and the captain were flying had taken off from Dubai, reached cruising altitude, and was overcome by a fire on board. The rapid spread of flames made the 747 uncontrollable. Thick, black smoke filled the cockpit, making it impossible for the pilots to see their instruments, just a few minutes after their first warning of a cargo fire. The fire damaged their oxygen and control systems and compromised communication with the tower. They were unable to land safely, and both men perished.

I sobbed. I looked from one man to another in total disbelief. I kept expecting the men to change their story, to give me some hope that Matt might still be alive. Angelina rubbed my back, not knowing what to say. The men's faces fought to stay emotionless, but I could see their agony twisting underneath. *Is this the first time they've had to deliver such news?* We were sitting out on the lanai on a hot and humid Florida afternoon. I was wearing a thick, zippered sweater, T-shirt, and jeans, and I was freezing. Everyone else was visibly sweating in short sleeves.

As the day wore on, more UPS employees came to my house, local pilots and administrative employees. They asked me to gather DNA samples from a toothbrush, hairbrush, or comb. It was really hard to do, not just emotionally, but because Matt had packed his toiletries for his trip nine days earlier. His hair was fine, blond, and short, too, so it was impossible to find a strand of hair. I sat on the bathroom floor, dug through Matt's things, and tried to make sense of everything. *Did someone actually tell me my husband is dead?* I felt extremely cold, and I seemed to be moving in slow motion.

I was asked to get his dental records. It was after five o'clock on the Friday of a holiday weekend. Our dentist, Katie, was also our friend, so I called her cell phone. She didn't answer, so I left a message explaining what happened and what I needed. I was grateful for not having to tell her the news directly. She was the first person I actually said those words to, although it was on her voice mail. Katie called shortly after. I hit Answer on the phone, and without saying hello, I handed it directly to the UPS employees to talk to her. I couldn't do it.

I next needed to call both sides of our family in Wisconsin. I called Matt's only sibling, Michelle, and asked if her husband, Ron was with her. I had to make sure she had someone there to support her. She said yes, so I choked out the news. She lives close to their mother, so I asked her to tell Nancy what had happened. Matt's father, Fred, had passed away eight years prior. I called my father and asked him to tell Mom, my one sister, and three brothers.

The people on the UPS Response Team asked if I'd like to go to Dubai the next day to see the crash site and then escort Matt's body home. "Yes, I want to." I felt very strongly about going on the trip, and I wasn't sure why. I knew without a doubt I'd regret it if I didn't go.

My neighbor and friend Gina picked up Ava from pre-K and brought her home to me. My poor little girl was confused and wondering what was going on. She sensed something bad had happened, but she didn't know what it was and apparently didn't want to ask.

At some point three grievance counselors arrived. I asked their advice on when I should tell Ava what happened. Two said wait a while; one said tell her right away. I decided to tell her when I returned from Dubai. She was smart and intuitive, and she deserved to know the truth.

Night fell, and everyone except Angelina slowly left the house. I brought Ava to sleep with me. I lay in bed, rubbed her back, and looked around the dimly lit room. I couldn't believe that my husband was dead. I could not comprehend it. My head filled with a strange, heavy ache, as if my brain was expanding and pushing against the interior of my skull.

I tried to talk to Ava to offer some sort of comfort. She looked off into nowhere, eyes wide open and filled with confusion and fear. I kept trying to say something, but no words came. I was only making odd, unrecognizable noises. They were strange sounds, like an animal's groans, an animal in tremendous and critical pain. I had never heard a human being make the noise before, but I heard it coming from me.

4

September 4, 2010

The next day, the house was again filled with people. UPS employees, family, friends, and neighbors stopped by. People brought coffee, water, and all sorts of food. My brother and sister-in-law came to take Ava to stay with them while I traveled to Dubai. Some of Matt's friends called to confirm the news was true and offered condolences. Matt's best friend, Scott, called from D.C., and I asked him to come to Dubai with Angelina and me. He agreed within seconds. UPS made the trip arrangements on a commercial airline. They assigned two escorts, Dave and Jeff, to see Angelina, Scott, and me through to Dubai and back.

On the flight that night, I took my first look at the pictures Matt had texted me from Dubai. They included the Burj Khalifa, the world's tallest building; the Dubai Aquarium, and a lollipop tree. It seemed the last two were both taken in a mall.

I couldn't believe I was going to Dubai. I didn't even know where it was until a couple weeks earlier, when Matt gave me a tutorial on the area and explained that UAE stood for United Arab Emirates. There are seven emirates, which we would call states, and Dubai is one of them.

I also looked at the YouTube video he had mentioned on the phone. It was of the Dubai Fountain lit up at night, with water shooting up and dancing in a pattern to the song "Time to Say Goodbye" sung by Andrea Bocelli and Sarah Brightman. It was beautiful yet haunting. Years before, we'd been given a CD of Italian-inspired instrumental music. I loved the music and played it over and over for years, not knowing there were words to it or even paying attention to the song title. To see the song title and hear the words was indescribably painful. It was eerie that he had sent the link to me about twelve hours before he died.

I understand the flight to Dubai was about fourteen hours from Atlanta. You could have told me it was two or thirty hours, and I wouldn't have known the difference. The fogginess of shock had rolled over me. I lost all concept of time, hunger, thirst, and need for sleep. I lost recognition of physical pain or discomfort or the ability to gauge the temperature around me.

I could not wrap my head around the fact that Matt was gone. I kept replaying the moment I was told he had perished, trying to make it make sense. *They came to my house and told me, so it must be true. It was on the news that the plane crashed and there are no survivors, so it must be true. I'm on my way to Dubai to see the crash site, so it must be true.*

It's as if you told me the sky was blue when I'd always believed it was orange. I could look up at the blue sky and think, *Yes, I see it's blue.* I could look at pictures taken a year ago of a blue sky and think, *Yes, it appears to have always been blue.* I could ask everyone I knew if the sky was blue and had always been blue. They could all answer, "Yes," but I still couldn't fully believe it was true. I had only a suspicion it might be.

I wondered if it was possible for everyone to be pulling a prank on me, yet I knew it would be far too cruel a prank to pull, plus the orchestration would have been nearly impossible.

I was unable to grasp such news, because the horror of it was too overwhelming. Shock was a gift that allowed me to grasp the news bit by bit.

We landed in Dubai at dusk and settled into our hotel rooms. The next day was Sunday, a working day there; their weekend is Friday and Saturday. I can't remember why, but we couldn't go to the crash site on Sunday or Monday. We stayed at the hotel while plates of local foods were brought to the room.

During this time, Scott and Angelina put me in a safe bubble. They handled all calls from friends and family to keep them up to date on what was happening. They handled the responsibility of either telling people for the first time or confirming the news that Matt had died. This selfless task must have been horrible for them. *Thank you, Angelina and Scott.*

A mall was attached to our hotel, and the three of us walked to it on Monday. Scott suggested I buy a gift for Ava, perhaps something with a ruby. The area is known for its rubies, and they are coincidentally Matt's birthstone. I looked at quite a few pieces of jewelry but couldn't buy anything. The last thing I wanted was to have a souvenir from the country that took my husband.

At night we drove into the city, saw the Burj Khalifa, and walked around the Dubai Fountain. The weather must have been warm, because everyone was fanning themselves. I was unable to gauge how warm it was, and I didn't feel discomfort. The whole city was elaborate and pristine; every sidewalk, door, building, and sculpture. It was a different world. Many families were out walking, shopping, and enjoying the evening together. The people were content and calm. I saw peacefulness and joy of life and family about them. I was a bit surprised and even disappointed, disappointed because I wanted them to be ugly people. I wanted to blame them for my husband's death.

I'd already decided I had every right to hate the Arabs because they were responsible; they took my husband from me. I thought of all the images of their hateful and criminal behavior I'd seen in the media. I couldn't wait to show my anger and disdain for them on their streets, but they were the exact opposite of what I expected to see. I watched all the couples with their little children. They were sweet and kind and loving toward each other. They were wonderful people.

I was overcome with shame. I was wrong in my eagerness to demonize them. That's how hatred and prejudice begin; that's how it blooms. I had first justified the incrimination in my mind and then gave myself the green light to condemn them. I was wrong.

We entered a mall and ascended to a second-floor restaurant that had a terrace overlooking the famous fountain. Cooled air was being piped up through the separated floorboards to provide relief from the heat. I could tell the YouTube video Matt sent me was taken from this vantage point. That night the fountain was dancing to Latin music. It didn't play "Time to Say Goodbye." I was relieved, because I was not sure how I would have reacted.

The next day was Tuesday, and we traveled to the crash site. We were asked to wear long pants and long-sleeved shirts to be respectful of the culture. The temperature was around 110°F.

We arrived at a dirt road in a field where the plane went down. From the van window I could see all the miraculously spared buildings that housed families. The plane wing first collided with a light pole. It was bent at a ninety-degree angle, lined up perfectly with the dirt road.

Immediately past the light pole were a couple very large divots in the ground where the plane hit and bounced. One quarter of a mile ahead was the actual crash site. Fortunately there was a naturally occurring knoll that obscured our view of the smoldering wreckage. I had no desire to see it close up.

A handful of men oversaw the site, because it was still under investigation. They met us at the van and cautioned us to walk only a short distance forward. Scott, Angelina, and I walked to the first ground impact point.

I dropped to my knees, crossed myself, and said a prayer for Matt. I also prayed for strength and courage for me, for Ava, and for everyone touched by the tragedy. Scott, in Jewish tradition, tore his shirtsleeve. We collected sand to seal in small jars for friends and family. I left a dozen red roses on the ground, Matt's favorite flower and the same type of flowers we had in our wedding.

I wasn't sure how long I knelt in the hot sand, but hours later, I noticed my knees were bright red. I wondered if they would blister. I also had no recollection of the smell of jet fuel at the crash site, but I was told it was overwhelming.

We returned to the van. I pulled the seat belt to fasten it, and it stuck. I almost burst into hysterical laughter, because the same thing always happened to Matt. For as long as I'd known him, he wrestled with every seat belt in every vehicle he ever sat in. It didn't matter which car or which seat he was in, the belt almost always stuck, and he'd rant. I'm sure he was just pulling it too quickly, but it always served as a great source of amusement. When my seat belt locked up, I felt strongly that Matt did it to let me know he was with me.

We returned to the hotel and started to pack for the evening flight home. The UPS escorts called me into a conference room to brief me on an update. They appeared apprehensive to tell me we would not be able to fly back with the remains. "The investigation is progressing, but the paperwork is not finished," Dave said.

"Okay," I replied coolly. They looked tense, and they continued to watch me as though waiting for more of a reaction. "I understand," I said and saw them relax, almost imperceptibly.

The news was not surprising; I had somehow known we wouldn't be flying back with his remains before we even left Orlando. I'd accepted the offer to fly to Dubai so I could see the crash sight. If I had believed we would fly back with

Matt's remains, I wouldn't have taken the trip. The thought of sitting through an interminable flight knowing his casket was somewhere on the same plane made me nauseated.

5

September 6, 2010

My brother brought Ava back to me. Scott and Angelina stayed with us the rest of the week. More friends, family, and neighbors came and went. Many beautiful flower arrangements arrived, and people brought casseroles, fruit, and other snacks. I was in shock and could not grasp the magnitude of what had happened, so I was puzzled by the deep concern everyone had for me. It was as if Matt's death pained them more than it did me. In truth, it did. They could fully comprehend what had happened, while I could not. My friends looked at me with love and sympathy. I knew if they could take even an ounce of my pain upon themselves, they would, without pause. The sorrow in my home was palpable. The rooms seemed darker and smaller.

My manager flew in from Texas to tell me I could take as much time as I needed. "How are you doing, Dawn?" he asked.

"I can't wait for it to be a year from now." I told him I knew the first year would be the hardest. I wanted to fall into a coma and fast-forward a year.

"Don't worry about next year. Worry about today, worry about this hour, and then the hour after that–just get through each day."

The comment didn't make sense to me and actually irritated me. I felt as if I were being corrected. *Wouldn't anyone want to slingshot ahead a year and forego the grief? Why are you correcting me?*

I now know that his advice was insightful and based on his own history with loss. I didn't realize how many harrowing days awaited me. I couldn't foresee the imminent and countless hours of agony and despair so intense that I would not be sure I could go on another five minutes.

Ava slept with me since my return from Dubai. One night I prepared myself to tell her that her father died. I wanted to use a softer phrase, such as "passed away," or "is no longer with us," or "we lost him," but those euphemisms would not work with a four year old.

I took a deep breath. "Ava, I know it has been very different around here the last couple of days. A lot of people have been coming over. Something really bad happened to your Dad. Ava…he died."

She drew in a sharp breath and stared at me with huge eyes. "How did he die?"

"There was a fire on his airplane, and it crashed."

"So he's not coming home?"

"No, he is with Jesus in heaven now."

She cried a little, but I knew she couldn't grasp what I'd told her. *Hell, I couldn't.*

6

September 12, 2010

It's a cruel waiting game for the repatriation date. The investigation in Dubai required all documents to be signed according to a mandatory sequence. If a document didn't get signed by a certain time of day, it couldn't go to the next stage until the next day.

Additionally, the emirate was celebrating the end of Ramadan (Eid), a national holiday that included non-working days, and it slowed the investigation severely. Frustrated does not even begin to describe how I felt. I received daily updates from my new stateside UPS escorts, Becky and Kristen, but the reports were mostly delay after delay.

I needed to plan Matt's funeral and reception, even though I didn't know the day or even month that it would take place. On Sunday, September 12, Ava and I flew to our home state of Wisconsin to make arrangements. Ava stayed with my parents, and I spent the next two days with my mother-in-law and sister-in-law.

I was numb and going through the motions. I did what had to be done, just checking off the list. We started at the cemetery and were directed to the two plots available near Matt's father, aunt, and grandparents.

I looked at the plots. "I'll take one of them."

The caretaker paused and then graciously asked, "Would you like both of them? Perhaps you would like to reserve the other one for your burial."

My head snapped up and I looked at him in disbelief. *Is he joking?* This a very disturbing question when you're thirty-nine years old. A sour taste filled my mouth and my throat felt thick. Practicality overruled, and I bought both plots. A few days later, I received the deed to my new land purchase, a sobering experience.

We continued to the church, met with the pastor, and chose the songs and verses for the funeral. Next we met with the funeral director and decided which photo and verse to be printed on the funeral program. I named the four groomsmen and two ushers from our wedding as honorary pallbearers.

I was removed from the experience, as if I were a different entity. It wasn't an out-of-body, looking-down-on-myself feeling. It was more like I had inhabited the body of someone I knew so I could help her. I knew she was in an immense amount of pain, yet I was guarded from it and could therefore get the work done for her.

I thought back to all the research I'd done in high school when I had a slight obsession with split personalities. I learned they are introduced during very traumatic experiences. The mind forms a new and separate personality to deal with the trauma. The newly created personality knows what the primary personality is experiencing and knows it's very painful, but the new personality feels little pain, if any at all, and usually takes on a protective role of the primary personality. *Is this what's happening to me?* The thoughts only served to amplify my fear of going insane.

I next had the responsibility to choose Matt's urn. Although he would be returned in a casket, I was told only ashes remained. Choosing an urn was a bizarre thing to do. *Which one would he prefer? How could he prefer one?* In the end, I pointed at a deep-green marble one, said "That one," and walked away.

The next day my mother-in-law, sister-in-law, and I met up again. We looked at a few venues for the reception. We drove to the Holiday Inn in Eau Claire, spoke with the sales department, and were told there was only one room that would meet our needs. Coincidentally it was the banquet room where Matt and I held our wedding reception fourteen years and six weeks earlier.

The banquet room held my blissful memories of our wedding dinner. That day it was empty, but as I looked across the room, I could picture it as it had been the night of our wedding reception. I could hear the din of the celebration and see the dance floor full of our guests. I looked toward the built-in bar and saw our friends circled around it, telling jokes and enjoying themselves. I saw my extended family filling the banquet tables, sharing stories, and catching up.

I could see Matt, handsome in his tuxedo, standing by his fraternity brothers. He looked over at me with an upward nod and a sly grin. He always made that gesture, a check-in with me, when we'd get separated at parties or other events packed with people. He did it because he was thinking of me and wanted me to know it. I loved the pure, unabashed thoughtfulness and care he always showed me.

I wanted the funeral reception to be there, in that very room, and I felt Matt would have wanted it that way too. I wasn't sure why. I guess it would've represented that our marriage had come full circle. The banquet facility turned out to be the busiest venue with the least flexibility. The sales staff gave us its limited days and times available and reminded us that someone else could book any one of the openings the next day. I asked for the banquet menu, and we left. I knew with complete certainty that the funeral reception would end up being there.

The last stop and by far the most painful emotionally was the flower shop. As I approached the entrance, excited chatter poured out of the store, growing louder with every step I took. It was packed with people choosing bouquets for weddings and baby showers. Everyone was planning happy events. Being in there, having to choose the flowers for Matt's funeral, almost brought me to my knees. He loved flowers and always spoiled me with beautiful arrangements throughout our marriage. He wanted me to feel special and be surrounded by beautiful things. There I was, buying flowers for him, and he was dead.

* * *

On the flight back to Florida, Ava and I were bumped up to the front-row seats in first class. Ava caught the flight attendant's attention because she looked so cute, swinging her little legs back and forth on the big seat. She was playing with her stuffed animal and singing softly.

The flight attendant and I chatted while Ava continued to sing, seemingly oblivious to our conversation. I asked her about the route she was flying and why she chose her profession. I was glad to have something new to talk about, with someone I didn't know. She innocently asked why we'd been in Wisconsin. Ava froze. *I guess she is listening after all.*

"Oh, just visiting family," I said.

7

September 15, 2010

We were back in Florida, and I kept Ava home from school for the rest of the week. Over the next two weeks, I got updates on the investigation and repatriation. The delays continued. My friends Carrie and Reeli spent a great deal of time with us and stayed over many nights. I swear I would not have eaten or thought to feed Ava had they not been there.

I was taking only necessary calls at that time, because I didn't want to talk to anyone. I was incredibly grateful for text messaging. It allowed me to respond immediately to everyone without uncomfortable pauses and having to answer, "How are you?"

Pete, one of Matt's good friends and a fellow pilot, started a Facebook page in Matt's name the day after the accident: www.facebook.com/MatthewC.Bell/UPS6. The immediate reach proved to be an invaluable tool in updating friends and family on any progress. It became a communal wall where people around the world could share pictures and memories, and it served as an outlet to express our mutual devastation, mercifully providing some level of comfort. *Thank you, Pete.*

The funeral home e-mailed a rough outline of Matt's obituary. It listed his birth and death dates and the high-lights of his education, military enlistment, and aviation career. It named the surviving family members and the details of the funeral. The article did a competent job, but it was cold and generic. It didn't speak to the man he was, his love for his family, or the reverence he had for life, so I decided to write his obituary. I sat at the computer over-whelmed with how to squeeze the entire life and essence of an amazing man into a few words. It was painful, but I did it, still feeling like it wasn't enough. It wasn't as great as I'd hoped, but it was the best I could do at the time.

Over the next two weeks, UPS continued to update me, but progress was sluggish. I nearly came out of my skin in frustration and sheer rage many times. It took everything I had not to scream and swear at everyone involved, even though they were as irritated as I was. I knew a tantrum wouldn't solve anything, but it would have felt good.

A couple women from the Human Resources Department at UPS flew in and personally brought me an outline of Matt's benefits. The list included his retire-ment accounts and life insurance policies, an education fund for Ava, and the Worker's Compensation package. The summary was invaluable, because I was unaware of all the policies Matt had selected. The women were also kind enough to highlight the benefits that had to be requested within a certain time frame, or they would become invalid. Without their help, I surely would have overlooked something and lost a valuable benefit Matt had chosen for Ava and me.

With nothing to do but wait for news, I began the administrative responsibilities of dealing with my husband's death. One day while I was looking over his insurance policies, my mind drifted back to a conversation Matt and I had at the beginning of the year, eight months prior. He told me he'd just paid the annual premium on a large personal life insurance policy he had taken out the month before Ava was born.

I was busy cleaning up the kitchen and only half listening at the time. I had no interest in discussing anything to do with the thought of his dying, and I was becoming a bit irritated. He persisted, and with a hint of pride told me how much money I'd get if he died, but that was Matt, always proud to provide for his family.

"What would you do with all of that money?" he asked.

I abruptly stopped cleaning and slapped my hands on the counter. I'd had enough of the conversation. *How could I even consider money, if it came to me only through his death? It sounded grossly like* The Monkey's Paw.

In *The Monkey's Paw*, a man is given the paw of a dead monkey. The paw is a talisman that can grant three wishes, but the requests are fulfilled in direful ways. The man wishes for a specific dollar amount and receives the exact amount in the form of life insurance issued as a result of his son's death.

My eyes met Matt's, and I spat at him, "I'd burn the money to have you back. That's what I'd do with it."

His jovial behavior immediately ended with my response. He cleared his throat and said softly, "Well, just so you know, if I die, everything you need is on the top shelf of the safe."

"Okay, good to know," I said flippantly, rolling my eyes to underrate the whole conversation.

I've heard stories of people who had absolutely no indication or reason to believe they were close to death, yet they prepared for it. They had gotten finances in order, detailed the funeral they wanted, tied up loose ends, and shortly after, they died from a previously undetected health malady or a car accident in which they had no fault. I wondered if somehow we knew, if somewhere deep in our subconscious or our soul, we sensed it. *Did Matt sense something ominous the morning of his death? Is that why he called me at a time when he would never have normally called me?*

* * *

Matt had handled the finances for the previous few years, so I had to get up to speed on everything. I started at the bank to get records of our checking, savings, and minor savings accounts. I braced myself as I walked up to the teller, explained the situation, and gave her my driver's license.

She entered my information in the computer and looked at me with shock and disbelief. "Was it Matt Bell? Do you have a little blond girl?"

Fighting to hold back emotion, I could only nod.

"He always brought her in here; he loved her so much," she said slowly and sadly, her eyes welling. "I'm so sorry."

I got the records, barely made it out to my car, and burst into tears.

Matt had such a big, gregarious personality. He exuded happiness and was chatty when taking care of business, whether in person or on the phone. His amiability unfortunately made it that much harder for me to tell businesses, doctors, lawn maintenance people, and others that he passed away. Everyone also knew he had a beautiful little girl, because he brought her everywhere and showed her off as much as possible. Many people I'd never met were saddened by the terrible news. He had a way of making people feel special by showing sincere interest in them and appreciation for the job they did.

I canceled his gym membership. I called the utility, phone, and credit card companies to get balances and payment due dates. I took his name off all the accounts. I never would have guessed how exhausting and painful the administrative job would prove to be. It required me to recount the tragedy over and over. I'd get the obligatory "I'm sorry for your loss," and then be transferred to another department, only to start over with why I was calling. After numerous transfers, I'd finally get a person instructing me to fax or mail in the death certificate. I spent one whole afternoon doing this drudgery, and I passed out from exhaustion once I'd finished.

One last, very important task was to make certain Ava had appropriate clothing for the repatriation ceremony and funeral. I stumbled through Macy's and found a simple, black A-line dress in her size. Trust me, there is nothing more heartbreaking than buying a dress for your four-year-old to wear to her father's funeral. It will truly test your faith.

8

Thursday, September 23, 2010

At 6:15 a.m., my UPS escort Becky called to tell me that Dubai was releasing the bodies. She and Kristen were coming to get us within an hour to fly to Louisville, Kentucky. The repatriation ceremony would be the next morning, twenty days after the accident.

I immediately sent a mass text message of the timeline to the rest of my family and friends and specifically to Pete, so he could update the Facebook page. My in-laws notified the pastor, funeral director, and florist. Gloria, the local UPS employee in Wisconsin, handled the details of the reception.

* * *

Ava and I, along with our escorts, arrived at the Louisville airport. A UPS employee picked us up and drove us directly to our hotel. My parents and mother-in-law, my sister-in-law, her husband, and their two boys were all flown in from Wisconsin. Scott, who had accompanied me to Dubai, flew in from D.C. Another of Matt's good friends, Major Daniel Schnick, USMC, was flown in from active duty in Australia. I had no idea how UPS and the USMC made that trip happen on such short notice, but someone at UPS did. I was grateful to have Dan there; it seemed right to have a friend in military uniform present at the repatriation. *Thank you, Dan.*

We were all very sad and greeted each other with heavy hearts. An odd mix of intense emotions hit me all at once. There was an initial blip of joy, because I saw the face of someone I cared about, and for just an instant, I focused on the person, not on what brought us there. That reaction was immediately replaced with a deep sadness for the loss we shared.

As much as I needed to be in everyone's company, I wanted to run away and shut myself in a small, dark room. I didn't want to face the fact that this situation was my life now, a life without Matt. Seeing everyone for the ceremony made it all the more real. I was no longer at home waiting for the news and fiddling with the possibility that maybe he'd come back alive. A part of me really thought that if there wasn't a funeral, he could come back to me.

Early the next morning, we all met in the lobby and were escorted to a hangar for the repatriation ceremony. The huge bay doors were wide open and the sun was rising on a beautiful September morning. Rows of chairs were lined up classroom-style facing the outdoors. The left side of the aisle was designated for the captain's family, friends, and coworkers. The right side was for us.

We were ushered to our seats, and I was thankful that someone at UPS had the foresight to put things under Ava's chair to keep her occupied. I saw a little book with crayons, some stickers, and a little brown teddy bear with the UPS shield embroidered on its chest.

Many administrative employees and pilots attended. When I arrived, most were sitting, but some mulled about and talked quietly. It was striking to see so many brown uniforms with gold bands circling the lower sleeves. *Big Brown*. Matt held the company in high regard. He thought UPS was one of the most well run companies in the world, and he started flight school with one goal in mind, to be a 747 captain at UPS. He believed the job would be the brass ring; it would be the pinnacle of his career. *He was so close.* He had just achieved first officer on the 747 a couple months earlier.

A stage and lectern were centered in front of our chairs. On each family's side was a large matted and framed picture of our pilot on an easel. Beautiful flower arrangements adorned the stage. I noticed Matt's picture but could not bring myself to look at it. I could only glance toward it out of the corner of my eye. It was an extremely emotional morning, and I tried hard to keep myself together. We sat and waited for the cargo plane to land. Everything was still, as if the wind, the birds, and the earth itself were waiting for the plane's arrival.

I heard it. The jet landed and was taxiing up to the left side of the hangar. My heart was beating so loud and so fast I could hear it in my ears. I thought the people behind me could hear it too. The plane taxied up far enough to allow the right wing to clear the hangar and took a gradual right turn to center in front of us. One thought turned over and over in my mind, *My husband's body is in there…my husband's body is in there.* It seemed unreal. I never thought he'd ever come home this way.

An elevating scaffold rose to meet the side cargo doors. The doors slowly rolled open. Two caskets, blanketed with American flags, were placed on the scaffolding, and the platform lowered to the ground. A six-man detail comprised of pilots, instructors, and managers was assigned to each casket. We rose from our seats as they stepped in time and guided the caskets in front of each respective family. I couldn't feel or hear my heart anymore. I wasn't sure if it was beating, if I was breathing, if I would be able to remain standing, or if I could keep my eyes open. I clenched my jaw, drew a deep breath, and braced myself to face Matt's return to me.

The detail centered on our row, and since I was by the aisle, the men and the coffin stopped diagonally to my right. I turned toward the coffin but could not make myself look at it. My gaze drifted above it, and I found myself looking directly at Matt's framed picture. His handsome, smiling face was looking right back at me. I heard, "Please be seated." I couldn't look away from his photo, the same photo I fought not to look at only moments before.

My thoughts were carried back to our wedding day, fourteen years earlier. I was at the back of the church in my big, beautiful dress, ready for my father to usher me to the altar. The rest of the wedding party had already walked down the aisle, and it was my turn. I was ridiculously happy; I couldn't wait to marry Matt Bell. *I can't wait to become his wife.*

The music cued and we started down the aisle. Everyone turned and smiled and slowly started to rise. Surprise shot through my body. *Why is everyone standing?* I had a moment of sheer panic. I thought something was wrong, because everyone was standing. My gaze darted to the altar. *I have to see Matt.* I needed to see his eyes. He was at the altar with the biggest smile on his face I'd ever seen. I had honestly never seen him look as happy as he did at that moment. I was immediately calmed by seeing him and then quietly laughed at myself for forgetting that everyone stands when the bride comes down the aisle.

Now I was in a hangar in Louisville looking over my husband's casket, and I was looking into his eyes and seeing his smiling face again, except this time it was a picture of him. Oddly enough, I was again immediately calmed, just as I had been walking down the aisle on our wedding day. I sensed that he was with me, and I felt comforted. I was struck with an understanding that as hard as this situation was and would be, I was going to be okay.

A man spoke at the lectern and was followed by another man who did the same. I was foggy on who they were and what exactly was being said, but I do remember they were sincerely sorry for what happened and they commended both pilots. The ceremony was then over. Everyone in our party was driven to another area with two small tents. One tent had snacks, drinks, and more toys for Ava.

The other tent was empty except for two short rows of chairs. I saw Matt's casket being placed inside and I was offered the opportunity to be alone with him. It was so awkward because I didn't think of him as being in the coffin. I walked into the tent and touched the glossy wood and whispered, "Until we meet again."

UPS had reserved a private jet to fly all of my family and the casket up to Eau Claire, Wisconsin, for a reception the company had arranged at the local airport. We landed and were met by many other family members and friends.

9

September 25, 2010

It was the day before the funeral, and I spent it visiting with family. I was in shock and on cruise control. I didn't cry even once; I just anxiously waited for the funeral.

That night I lay in bed and considered the impending funeral. *Should I say something there?* I wanted to offer some kind of memorial valediction. It wasn't to say farewell in a final sense, but more of a good-bye to the life he led.

In the morning I woke and immediately began writing. I quickly dressed and helped Ava get dressed. I explained to her that we were going to her father's funeral. She didn't know what I meant, because she had never been to a funeral. I described it as simply as I could. She didn't ask any questions; she didn't know what to ask.

We arrived at the church and learned that the florist mixed up the order and sent twice the flowers. I was not in the least bit upset and was actually quite delighted. Despite being such a guy's guy, Matt definitely appreciated beautiful flowers.

Ava played with her cousins while I stood in the receiving line, an act of self-torture, and I was not sure why I kept standing there, greeting person after person. It was uncomfortable because people did not know what to say other than they were sorry. The occasion was another one where my mind wasn't completely processing what I was doing or why I was doing it. I just fell back on following tradition that called for me to welcome people arriving at the event.

I was wearing a dress and a pair of shoes with heels that were about three inches high. I wore the same type of heels daily at work, so it was nothing out of the ordinary for me, but person after person commented on my heels and expressed concern for my comfort. One of my aunts even asked me what size I wore and offered to exchange my heels for her flats. This concern baffled me, because I had no concept of how my feet, my legs, or my entire body, for that matter, was feeling. I wondered if people said such things because they didn't know what else to say.

I was aware of exactly what had happened and where I was, but again felt removed from it. I could not deal with the magnitude of being at my husband's funeral. It's hard to explain. I knew it was a sad occasion, and I felt sadness, but it wasn't intense. I again felt I had inhabited someone else's body, so I reverted to my usual behavior of smiling and asking how everyone was, despite being filled with bewilderment.

The service was beautiful. So many people attended that extra chairs had to be brought in. Most of Matt's fraternity brothers sat in one section, the family sat in another section, and UPS was well represented in another area. Ava chose not to sit with me and instead sat on my close friend Reeli's lap in the row behind me. I asked Ava a couple times if she'd like to sit with me, but she said "No." She was so overwhelmed she wasn't sure what to do. *Thank you, Reeli.*

My sister-in-law Stacey had put together a fantastic slideshow full of pictures of Matt through the years. Some were of him with waist-length hair from high school; some showed fun-filled times with his fraternity brothers, and some were of the many vacations he and I had taken. Most are of him and our families or just him enjoying life through the years. *Thank you, Stacey.*

Our friend Scott stood to deliver the eulogy. I watched as he walked up to the altar and inhaled a deep breath. He crossed his arms in a protective stance and steeled himself to speak to everyone of this friend who meant so much to him. His words were beautiful, and he captured Matt's life through the years. I realized that everyone except perhaps his mother and sister learned something new about Matt, because no one person had been there to witness every phase of his life.

Scott shared that he met Matt when they were teenage pledges to the Phi Gamma Delta fraternity. They were an odd pair but soon became the closest of friends. He spoke of Matt's love of his parents, his sister Michelle, and her subsequent family. He told of Matt being a proud papa and how he spoiled his daughter he was so proud of.

He recounted Matt's dogged determination and unwavering persistence when he set his mind to something, whether it was his career path or marrying the woman he loved. He shared how Matt was drawn to associations with a strong sense of connection between the individual members, such as their fraternity, the Masons, and the US Marine Corps. I do not know how Scott delivered this message without falling apart. *Thank you, Scott.*

I didn't have the same strength and could not read what I wrote that morning. The pastor agreed to read it for me.

> They say that when you laugh, the world laughs with you, but when you cry, you cry alone. Today that is simply not true. There are people crying all over the world today, and they are not alone. We all cry because the world has lost a great man, a great husband, a great father, a great brother, a great son, and a great friend.
>
> Matt held a position that allowed him to meet people all over the world, and he always made an impression. People remembered Matt because he was kind and respectful and had a sincere interest in meeting them and asking them how their day was going.
>
> It is tragic that our Ava will not have her father by her side as she grows, and it is tragic that I will not have my husband, who was the perfect complement to me. He truly made me the person that I am today, and I feel I have lost half of me.
>
> Matty, I will honor you and your memory by being thankful for the years we had you and not being angered by the years we will not.
>
> But for now I must say good-bye, and it is with an indescribable ache in my heart that I say, Good night, my prince.

The funeral ended, and we proceeded to the cemetery on a beautiful sunny afternoon, the opposite of the gray, rainy day that had been forecasted. As Matt's urn was lowered into the ground, I felt an unexpected relief. It was the slightest buoy to the intensity of the past twenty-three days.

The reception followed at the Holiday Inn, right where our wedding reception had been. The hall was available after all, even on short notice. I couldn't help smiling when I looked at the built-in bar surrounded by Matt's fraternity brothers, all dressed in suits and drinking Heineken just as they had done fourteen years earlier.

The occasion was clearly not the joyous one our wedding had been, but on this sad day, the people I wanted and needed to be with once again surrounded me. It's important to attend funerals to acknowledge one's life and death and confirm solidarity with those who share your loss. I'm very grateful to everyone there that day for the concern and respect they showed to Matt and our family.

10

Monday, September 27, 2010

A va and I boarded a plane to return to Florida. She and I were in the aisle congested with everyone else trying to get to their seats. Ava was being uncharacteristically rude and bumping into people. She sassed back when I corrected her. I admit I wasn't trying too hard, because I was completely exhausted, and I knew her behavior was very abnormal for her. She was only reacting to what she had been through.

An older woman turned around sharply with a look of obvious irritation. I was sure she thought Ava was a terribly undisciplined child and I was an absent mother. I was overcome with an intense wave of aggression; my heart was pounding and adrenaline raced through me when I observed her judgmental scrutiny of Ava.

I glared at her and silently dared her to make a nasty comment. *C'mon, say it; say one word.* I wanted to fight. I wanted to scream. I wanted to debase and humiliate her. I wanted her to know she was criticizing a little girl who had buried her father the day before. I wanted to attack someone

- everyone. I wanted to release an ounce of the rage I felt. My body seemed to enlarge physically and my senses sharpened. I was ready to strike. I could have taken on a lion. She was as unsuspecting as a butterfly floating toward an electric fence. *Say something snotty. Do it! Look at me!*

Fortunately for both of us her face softened, she turned back around, and moved toward her seat. The hostility that had taken a fraction of a second to overcome me seeped away at a snail's pace.

The plane landed in a downpour. I ached to get home to return to some sense of normalcy.

Ava and I settled on the couch and curled up under a tied fleece blanket my manager's wife made for us. I turned on the TV but could not get a cable channel to come on. Little Ava was becoming anxious because she wanted to snuggle with her mom and watch a favorite Disney show.

I didn't know what to do, but a message appeared on the screen instructing me to contact my provider and relay a specific message code. I called and reached a customer service representative, explained the situation, and gave her the message code. She told me with disdain that the account had not been paid, and I would not get the channels back until I did pay. I told her that my husband normally took care of the bills and I had no idea the bill had not been paid. She could not mask her disgust as she informed me that numerous e-mails had been sent warning us that the account was past due. She added that it was unlikely that I didn't know the account was overdue.

I was reeling with disbelief that someone could be so rude and basically call me a liar. I'd updated all our accounts and was paying all the bills, but this one had slipped through the cracks. It was billed electronically and went directly to the one e-mail account I didn't check. Initially I had no intention of going into detail about my situation with the customer service representative. I wanted one night without speaking of Matt's death or funeral, but I had to tell her why the bill hadn't been paid. I said with a shaking voice that my husband recently passed away and I mistakenly overlooked the cable bill. She replied, "Yes, I'm sure he did," with such condescension I nearly dropped the phone. I ignored her and paid with a credit card.

I think the channel came back on immediately; I really don't recall. I just remember being stunned by the realization that someone actually thought I manufactured a story about my husband's death to get my cable turned back on. Cable! My brother works for a different cable company and later told me that unfortunately, such things happened a lot. Some people will say anything to get their cable turned back on.

11

Late September 2010

I stayed in the blessed blanket of shock throughout September. I rarely cried but for a few jags. Tears came occasionally and I wept a little, but it wasn't anything like the wailing and howling I expected.

One time I forced myself to stare at Matt's picture. I willed myself to cry, to feel something for my loss, but I couldn't. I felt only shame and confusion and I questioned whether I even missed him. *What is wrong with me?*

In truth, I still could not fully believe he died, in part because of the protective nature of shock, but also because I had nothing more tangible than a divot in the Dubai ground and an urn that had been buried with his ashes, ashes I didn't even see. I wasn't there when the accident occurred on the other side of the world. I didn't identify his body or see his remains.

Matt was an international cargo pilot. His work schedule was a cycle of flying two weeks and then being home for two weeks. I was used to his absence. A big part of me expected him to walk in the door any minute, ready to begin his two-week break at home.

My friend Renee called one evening and asked how I was doing. I assured her I was fine and added an impudent comment such as "People die every day."

She responded gently, "Yes, they do, but they're not all your husband."

I knew she was right, but what I couldn't put into words was that I was disturbed by my inability to cry and my lack of grief, and I was embarrassed to admit it. I tried to match my words to my actions and treat death like it was just a fact of life.

I continued to feel like I was outside of my own body, because I couldn't feel what I should have been feeling mentally or physically. Sitting down, I wasn't aware of the sensation of the chair against my body. I couldn't perceive the weight of a glass in my hand. In the shower I knew water was falling on me and I was getting wet, not because I sensed the water hitting me, but because I knew it was a cause-and-effect action.

I was unaware of the space my body occupied. I changed my clothes and saw the outsides of my thighs covered in hard knots in various stages of bruising. I didn't feel the pain and then look down at my legs. I noticed the injuries only because my eye was drawn to the green, blue, and yellow colors of the bruises. I was confused by their origin, but later realized I'd been walking too close to tables and countertops. I'd been hitting the pointed corners over and over again. Not once did I recognize the pain when it happened.

My adrenaline was in overdrive. I had no appetite or thirst, as if I'd become a machine that didn't need to eat or drink anymore. For months my underarms smelled of acrid sweat that was so concentrated I had to throw away numerous T-shirts because the smell would not wash out. I could not mask or inhibit the distinctive and wretched smell with deodorant. *Is this what an animal smells when it smells fear?*

My escalated metabolism, coupled with a lack of eating, resulted in rapid weight loss. The weight was taken completely from my fat stores, because my lean muscle didn't deteriorate at all. In truth I had the most muscular definition I'd ever had in my life.

I rarely slept, and if I did, it was only in short spurts. I was tormented by images of Matt struggling to land that plane. The last minutes of his life must have been filled with indescribable terror, knowing he didn't have a chance. *Did he scream in fear? Did he call out to me?*

I experienced severe dehydration and electrolyte imbalance. I was racked with incredibly painful foot cramps that also woke me throughout the night. My vision became distorted and wobbly from a lack of fluids, before I thought to drink something.

You might think the assault on my body would make me a zombie, unable to accomplish anything, but it was quite the opposite. I never felt grogginess from lack of sleep. My senses toward the outside world were actually more acute. I could hear and discern sounds at a distance I didn't believe I ever had before. Smells were sharper, and my body felt strong, strong in a sense that I could protect myself or run from a physical threat, if necessary.

I had returned to caveman days, when humans were living in a world full of potential danger. My body knew my mind was compromised and responded by enhancing my senses to keep me alive. I was in self-preservation mode and operating on all reserves. I was undistracted and unrestricted by physical needs, so I could focus solely on survival.

12

Early October 2010

The local insurance agent who held one of Matt's life insurance policies called to let me know the check had arrived. We decided to meet the next morning at a nearby Starbucks. I arrived first, ordered coffee, and sat down. He arrived shortly after, introduced himself with a big smile, and turned to get his coffee. He was surprisingly outgoing and very friendly. He was spirited, as if he had just gotten good news or something. His demeanor toward me did not match that of anyone else who knew of the loss I'd just suffered.

He returned to the table and talked to me as though we were old friends meeting under happy circumstances. He asked questions about me and my interests. He actually seemed flirtatious. *No, this can't be.* I chided myself for even thinking such a thing. He told me about his wife and their grown son who worked with him. He continued chatting amiably and asked me what I had planned for the day.

"I don't know; maybe I'll see a movie. I don't feel like being home today."

"I'd love to see a movie with you," he said.

What is happening? The man could not possibly be hitting on me, but his behavior was odd. As the conversation continued, it became apparent that yes, he was hitting on me.

I thanked him for delivering the insurance check and left quickly. The encounter was the single most disgusting one I had with anyone following Matt's death. I wondered with revulsion if he'd ever succeeded at taking advantage of other vulnerable women.

13

Second Week of October 2010

When the accident first occurred, the local police were notified. Officers stopped by my house and asked how I'd like them to respond. I felt anxious because of the circumstances and the sensationalism that always surround a plane crash. I worried that a reporter would show up on my doorstep to "get the exclusive." I asked the police department to drive by the house once or twice a week for the first couple of months.

On a Saturday in October, Ava and I planned to visit my brother and his family an hour from us. We were in the garage and about to leave. The garage door was open and both of us were in the idling car. I was twisted around the console trying to see the DVD controls in the backseat to get a movie to play for Ava on the trip. With my limited technical abilities, the process took some time.

I was startled by the sound of a slap on my car window. I instantly untwisted, surprised to see a policeman standing in my garage.

"Can you step out of the car?" he asked.

I opened the door thinking I'd done something wrong but couldn't imagine what it could be. He stood close to my door, so when I stepped out, I was forced to stand quite close to him.

He was in my personal space and not backing up. He kept staring into my eyes as if expecting to see something. He asked, "Who are you, and what are you doing?"

"I'm Dawn Bell. I live here, and I'm trying to get my daughter's movie to play before we drive to my brother's house in Lakeland."

He kept watching me intently and then looked past me into the car at Ava. He looked her over, as if to make sure she was okay. He looked back at me and studied me again. I began to feel incredibly uncomfortable.

Suddenly his whole demeanor changed, he backed up a step, and he relaxed. "How are you doing? Has anyone bothered you since your husband's accident?"

"No, we haven't been bothered at all. Thank you for watching over us."

"That's our job, ma'am, but if anything comes up, let us know immediately, okay?"

He turned to leave and added, "Have a safe trip."

What was that all about? I later realized he was making sure we were physically unharmed. Imagine the scenario; a woman who recently lost her husband is in her car idling in the garage. She's twisted around leaning into the back-seat area and looks like she may have passed out from asphyxiation. I later realized he was making sure my eyes weren't dilated, I could speak coherently, and that my story checked out.

14

Mid-October 2010

In the week or two before my return to work, I read through a multitude of greeting cards sent by many thoughtful people. People also sent helpful gifts, including blankets, journals, and a number of books on dealing with the death of a loved one. Two of the books were duplicates, both from the same national bookstore. I had the receipts, so I decided to return some of them.

The clerk helping me said he couldn't give me a refund because company policy allowed returns only within thirty days of purchase. Verging on tears, I told him that they were gifts in response to my husband's death the previous month, and I was sent two copies of each.

He shrugged with disinterest and said he was going to have to check with his manager to see if I could get an in-store credit. I walked away in a daze. *Forget it; I'll donate them.* I thought back to the customer service representative at the cable company who was so thoughtless too. I had to believe these incidents were uncommon, because people would not be as insensitive if they knew I was telling the truth.

I continued through the same mall to return a shirt I had purchased for Matt a month before his death. The employees at that store were incredibly accommodating and thoughtful.

I left the mall and drove to my dental appointment. It may seem odd that I was returning books and clothes and going to the dentist, but I didn't know what else to do. I just did what I would normally do. I considered everyone at my dentist's office to be a friend; otherwise I probably would've canceled that appointment.

Everywhere I went I saw people going about their business as if it were any other day. I envied their carefree manner. I felt like screaming at the gas station and grocery store, "Why are you acting like nothing's happened? Don't you know who just died? My husband! The greatest person to have ever entered my life is dead."

* * *

I filled out the last of Matt's life insurance claims and sent it in to the company's New York office. A representative assigned to the case called shortly after and informed me that the claim required an investigation, since the policy had been purchased fewer than two years before the policy holder's death. It had been one year and eight months and was the largest claim Matt purchased.

"Is there a question as to the circumstances of his death?"

"It's company policy, ma'am. A private investigator will call you shortly. You need to be cooperative and completely honest with your answers, or you could be charged with a punishable offense." *Have I just been accused of something?*

I wasn't sure how long the investigation would take and considered how dreadful the delay would be if I needed the money to pay my bills. I couldn't imagine that stress on top of everything else.

A couple days later, a kind and respectful investigator named Ed called me. He requested that I provide the names and contact information of any doctors who had treated Matt within the previous five years as well as the pharmacies that had filled his prescriptions. Ed asked if Matt had a good driving record; any arrests; any tobacco, drug, or alcohol use; and if he'd ever been in a rehabilitation facility.

He asked about Matt's physical health, if he'd participated in hazardous sports, whether our marriage was happy and stable, and if Matt was a happy person or tended toward depression. He asked me about my job, when Matt and I met, when we married, and if we had children. He finished by asking how many life insurance policies Matt had and how much each was worth.

He recorded all my answers, and a few days later he mailed me a typed statement summarizing our phone conversation. I was instructed to review it for accuracy and sign it with a witness present. I was also sent authorizations for the release of medical records and an affidavit of legal next of kin I was required to sign in the presence of a notary public.

The forty-five-minute phone call, followed by reading the statement and getting forms signed in front of a witness and notary public, was unbelievably exhausting. It doesn't seem like it would have taken a lot of time or energy, but these few tasks drained me completely.

The investigation dragged on for months. I continually called the representative to get updates, but I met with delay after delay. Adding to the frustration, I was never actually able to speak to the representative directly, only his assistant.

I told my friend Scott about the complicated and time-consuming insurance procedures, and he said not to worry; every day the payment was delayed, the company was required to pay me interest. *What, really?* I did some research and learned the information was true; not in all states, but it was true in Florida. I called the insurance company the next morning and asked the representative's assistant to be sure the interest was included with the benefit check whenever it was issued. She said, "No, payment of interest applies to only certain states, and Florida isn't one of them."

I told her my research contradicted hers, but she remained adamant on the point. I asked her to send me literature that supported her position. About a week later I received a thick envelope filled with insurance benefit guidelines and statutes. The verbiage was a bit over my head, but I understood enough to know nothing in the packet pertained to paying interest on a delayed claim. It was odd her cover letter was handwritten on letterhead and simply stated, "Here is the information you requested." *Nothing like covering your tracks.*

I immediately called the company and told the assistant what she sent me was garbage, and I expected interest on my claim. I demanded to speak to her manager within twenty-four hours, or I would file a claim against them for delay of payment and the company's illegal attempt to avoid paying interest on a claim filed more than four months prior.

The very next morning the representative himself called and told me my benefit check was being processed as we spoke and he would personally ensure it was overnighted to me. He also confirmed interest on the delay was due and would be paid in a separate check to be issued that day and sent through regular mail.

How awful that the insurance company preyed upon me in my weakened state. When a person is stricken with grief, the smallest task requires a staggering amount of energy, especially if it involves unfamiliar information and terminology. I'm sure the company banked on my being unable to fight, even if for a few months, so it could continue to earn interest on money that was rightfully mine.

15

Third Week of October 2010

Neither Matt nor I had prepared a will or trust, and getting mine done had become a priority. I wanted to declare legally what steps would be taken for both Ava and me if I became incapacitated or incompetent or if I died. I also needed help in understanding what steps had to take place following Matt's death, in regard to his estate. I was thankfully referred to a brilliant, honest, and kind probate attorney named John Moran, of Dunlap & Moran in Sarasota, Florida.

John explained in full detail all the estate planning documents I needed. These included a last will and testament, revocable trust agreement, durable power of attorney, living will declaration, designation of health care surrogate, pre-need declaration of guardian, and medical release authorization form.

He also opened an estate for Matt, which allowed all companies or people who believed Matt either owed them money or was delinquent on an account an opportunity to make a legal claim for payment. After a certain amount of time, in my case it was just a little more than two years, John closed the estate, and I was no longer responsible for any future claims.

Additionally, John alerted me to two critical benefits I was not aware of. First, any of Matt's outstanding student loans would be absolved; I needed only to send Sallie Mae a letter and death certificate. I did so, and a couple of months later, the entire debt was forgiven.

Second, I was eligible for Social Security benefits, a monthly check based on the decedent's lifetime earnings, to be used to support surviving family members for a specific number of years. I'd always thought I had to be retired to receive Social Security benefits, but no, I was eligible when my spouse passed away, regardless of my age. John instructed me to apply for this benefit at my local Social Security Administration office.

16

Fourth Week of October 2010

Time stood still but somehow passed. I didn't feel hunger, so I lacked the cue to gauge mealtime. I didn't feel sluggish from low blood sugar levels that would normally happen to me in mid-afternoon. I was still in a black hole that did not allow me to comprehend time or space.

I could not grasp the phrase *next week*. Before Matt's death, if someone said next week or next August, I could visualize the calendar month and know what I had scheduled. Now I could hardly fathom *tomorrow*. If I tried to picture next week, only darkness filled my head. A black screen was all I saw.

The worst part about being unable to focus on a future date was that it negated my formerly useful coping mechanism. In the past, when going through a tough spot in my life, I looked at the calendar, saw the current day and picked a day in the future when everything would be better. The day was always arbitrary, chosen completely at random, but I picked a day, circled it, and focused on it. I told myself over and over that everything would be better on that day.

Every inch of me believed on the day I circled, my troubles would be gone. The great thing was that my problems were always better on the day I circled, really. If not completely better, things were significantly better.

I couldn't use that coping mechanism any longer. Calendars seemed like odd tools I'd never used before. Tomorrow didn't compute. I seemed to have no future at all. I've read since that an inability to construct a future is a symptom of depression. If I was depressed, I didn't know it. I was still in the protective vacuum of shock, but it was about to end.

17

Early November 2010

Shock slowly dissipated over a handful of days and was replaced with an all-consuming grief. It enveloped me like thick, cold, murky ink. I was unable to quantify just how sad I was, but I knew it was a level I'd never reached before. I cried constantly, so much so that I couldn't imagine it was possible to produce more tears, but I did. I was thoroughly exhausted at all times, and unable to sleep more than an hour or two in succession. The strongest prescribed sleep medications did not help. Day and night I was tortured by the irreversibility of Matt's death.

Every inch of my body ached. My heart physically hurt, as if a spike had been driven through it and pinned me to the ground. I felt paralyzed and prayed every day for my heart to stop beating so I could finally stop hurting, but it wouldn't stop beating. My chest felt snapped in a giant mousetrap, and I was being kept alive in someone's sadistic game. A dull ache permeated my arms, legs, back, neck, and head. I had been handed a life sentence of pain, *but what are the charges?*

I had used my entire supply of bereavement, vacation, and sick days. I returned to work as a pharmaceutical sales representative calling on pediatricians. The one saving grace was that I'd known these doctors for only a few months. Many providers were just now recognizing me when I walked in, and only a few knew my name. No one put together that I was the wife of one of the pilots in the plane crash. I was saved from having to speak of it all day, every day. The reprieve provided an unexpected bit of escape; for part of my days, I could pretend nothing bad had happened.

I was a danger on the road. I mistakenly went the wrong way on a one-way street. I was oblivious to red lights and blew through them. I was disoriented and got lost driving to offices I'd visited before. I was inefficient coordinating my day and kept misplacing the sales tools I needed to perform my job. I lost all interest in promoting my medications. *The doctor hasn't tried my new acne medication once in the last month? Who cares? At least his wife isn't dead.*

I continued to be ambivalent at the thought of my own death. Waiting with my blinker on to turn left into my neighborhood, I saw a semi driving toward me up the two-way road. I tinkered with the thought of pulling out in front of him, but I knew I wouldn't. Instead I watched him approaching and begged him to lose control and barrel straight into me. I even unbuckled my seat belt, I suppose to emphasize my request. I wanted him to fall asleep for just a millisecond and plow me over.

I still could not comprehend time. My senses and instincts were numb. I felt like a victim of a severe head injury that rendered me incapable of properly caring for my daughter or myself. I was floating in a fog and couldn't clearly remember things that happened the day before. Thoughts circled and scattered in my head, unable to form a logical pattern. I could not focus or think anything through to a conclusion. I felt frantic and panicky, because I didn't know what was going on. My brain could not assess my environment. It was a malfunctioning calculator trying to add numbers, but unable to reach a sum. It wasn't giving me any reassurance that I wasn't in danger, so I didn't know if I was or not. I was filled with constant fear and anxiety.

The months of self-neglect were taking a toll. Ridges formed on my nails from malnutrition. My formerly healthy, soft skin became dry and blotchy. My hair thinned and dulled. My gums were sensitive and bled when I brushed my teeth. I developed an irritation around my lower lip marked by intense swelling and redness. The skin became raw, flaky, and extremely painful to the touch. An icepack and medication provided little relief.

I tried to eat. The act of chewing seemed foreign, as though I were doing it for the first time and with someone else's teeth. My body rejoiced at the hint of a meal and flipped on every hunger signal full bore, begging me to eat everything in sight, but I refused, because I knew the pain that would follow if I did. My stomach had shrunk drastically over the past few months and my intestines had collapsed. Painful abdominal cramping followed every bite as food moved through my digestive tract. Enzymes attacked each morsel of food like piranha to chum. As much as I knew I needed to eat, I wouldn't. It simply was not worth the pain. I wondered if I'd ever want to or be able to eat normally again.

Every day was silhouetted by an absence of joy. I was indifferent toward everything. I had no interest in music, movies, or my favorite television shows. I had minimal concern for my friends, my cats, and even my daughter. Each day I finished work and picked Ava up from pre-K. I didn't ask her how her day was, because honestly, I didn't care.

We drove home and I'd lie on the sofa while she played at her craft table near me. I watched her as she colored, and I tried to force myself to regain a fraction of the unshakable devotion I had for her just months before, but it wouldn't come.

"Mommy, do you want to color with me?"

"No, honey. Mommy's got a headache."

"Didn't you have a headache yesterday?"

"Yeah, I did. I think I'm sick. Maybe I can color tomorrow."

I scolded myself. *She lost someone too. Help her! This isn't all about you. Get off your pathetic ass and play with her, talk to her. You'll regret it if you don't.* But I couldn't. I just couldn't. I gave her everything I had, but sadly, it wasn't much.

I microwaved macaroni and cheese and added canned fruit to her plate for dinner, a far cry from the healthy, homemade meals with fresh produce I used to serve. I sat with her while she ate. I picked at the skin around my fingernails until it bled and ate nothing. In silence, I helped her put on her pajamas and brush her teeth. I could tell she was looking at me in the mirror as I brushed her hair, but I didn't look back at her. I was ashamed of my behavior, but

I couldn't change it. I read her the shortest book I could find. We said our prayers and kissed good night, and I shut off her light.

I returned to the sofa and stared off into nothing. I had begun drinking two or three glasses of red wine every night, excessive for me, but I never suffered a hangover the next day, or if I did, I couldn't discern the discomfort as being any different from what I was constantly feeling. I'd never taken any illegal drugs, but I imagine if I had, I would have turned to them, *anything to help dull the wretched pain.*

One night I mixed wine with a prescription sleeping pill and didn't remember going to bed. The next morning I was confused at seeing bubble wrap strewn across the floor and an opened box inside my front door. Apparently I shut off the home alarm, brought a delivered package of olive oil inside, opened it, relocked the door, and reset the alarm. I had no memory of any of those things, and it deeply frightened me. I worried that if I could do such things with no memory of it, what else might I do? In that condition could I hurt myself? Would I hurt my daughter?

* * *

People tried to mask a look of surprise when they saw what was happening to my appearance. They were concerned, but I put on a good show. I kept Ava fed and in clean, ironed clothes. I showered regularly, retrieved my mail daily, and set my garbage on the curb. I continued to decorate for holidays, which was mostly for Ava, but it benefited me too. It kept the worriers away.

When I ran into a neighbor or someone I knew, I'd put up a strong front. I instinctively stood up straight, spoke evenly, maintained direct eye contact, and held my face emotionless. I acknowledged that I was sad and I missed Matt and I was the best I could be without him. I said what I was supposed to say, so people left me alone, which was exactly what I wanted.

The worst encounters were with people who picked at me with question after question. Those people weren't my close friends; they were acquaintances or distant family members. It was sick really, how they kept at me or said something inappropriate to get a reaction. They wanted me to break down; they wanted to see my agony on display in front of them. It seemed they gained a sadistic sense of satisfaction from someone else's pain. They reminded me of the demented audience at a gladiator ring, or those who wrung their necks to look at accident scenes on the interstate.

Putting on a charade was exhausting. I was sick of my plastered smile and of reassuring everyone that I was hanging in there. I was sick of acting strong when I could barely function, but the alternative was worse.

I wasn't isolating myself to be devious; I just couldn't stand the awkwardness of being with others. I was tired of being asked how I was or if there was something someone could do. I couldn't handle the sad eyes, the faces full of pity, seeing their worst nightmare right in front of them. I hated being the one whose life nobody wanted.

Only my closest friends knew the depths of my sadness, but I kept even them from knowing the whole truth. I never told anyone I ignored my daughter and was too stern with her, that I was drinking more than I should, or that I wished my life would end.

What if they called the Department of Children and Families and they took my daughter away from me? I couldn't lose her too. In my right mind, I knew such a thing would never happen, but in my grieving mind, my thoughts were deranged.

18

Friday, November 12, 2010

I did a web search and learned the local Social Security Administration building was relatively close to me. The website suggested I set up an appointment and state my need to expedite the process. I did so and was directed to a list of forms to bring, which included a copy of the death certificate, our marriage license, my birth certificate, and Ava's birth certificate.

I arrived early, checked in at a kiosk screen, and pulled a number. The room was a lot like the Department of Motor Vehicles, a government facility with drab colors and uncomfortable chairs set up theater style. I heard muffled conversations between people whose numbers had been called and the tellers, who mostly stared at their screens without looking up. My gaze settled on a television affixed to the wall, although I was completely unaware of what was airing.

I drifted back to a visit shortly after Matt's and my wedding day. We went together to get my new driver's license with my surname change. I was giddy with excitement, like a five-year-old on Christmas morning. The room was crowded with people that day, and it was taking forever for my name to be called, but I didn't mind. I relished every minute I sat with my husband. *My husband.* I loved calling him that.

Finally I heard, "Dawn Bell" over the speaker, and I jumped up and screamed, "Yes!" as if I'd been called as the next contestant on *The Price is Right*. I hurried across the room to get my new ID. I grabbed it too quickly off the printer, and the still-hot plastic made me drop it, giggling. Matt was sincerely flattered by my enthusiasm and called me by my full name for weeks. I couldn't hear it enough.

I snapped back to the present day, when once again, someone called, "Dawn Bell." I was led to an area in the back and motioned to sit down. I was an emotional mess that morning. I'd just finished my second week back at work and was exhausted. It hadn't occurred to me to have a friend accompany me, so I was alone and very fragile. I prayed the interview wouldn't take long.

The benefits coordinator knew my reason for the appointment and was cautious and thoughtful in asking for information. I barely answered three questions before I fell apart. I couldn't stop crying, and my sobs shook my whole body. I was creating a scene that mortified me. My nose ran, and I rifled unsuccessfully through my handbag for a Kleenex. Genuine sympathy flooded the clerk's face and she bolted for a box of tissues.

She sat patiently while I tried to pull myself together. I didn't know how long I sat and cried, but she assured me there was no rush. She gently encouraged me to let it out.

She glanced at me with concern but was kind enough not to stare at me in my meltdown. I could sense other people looking my way to see what was going on, and some gawked at me. I was horrified. I saw the clerk shoot a look that said, "What are you looking at?" until they all turned away. Such protectiveness from a total stranger astounded me.

I finally composed myself and finished answering the questions. Later I learned that in my distress, I'd mistakenly transposed the routing numbers on the checking account where my benefits were to be directly deposited. My mistake delayed my first payment for months, which would have been devastating were I not in a good financial situation.

On that day, however, I returned to my car and called my manager at work. I could barely speak when I tried to explain that I couldn't go out in the field that day, not in my condition. He mercifully granted me a day off and told me to go home and take care of myself. *Thank you, Bill.*

19

Mid-November 2010

Ava and I began to attend New Hope for Kids, a family grief-counseling center. The kids were grouped by age and met upstairs, while the adults convened downstairs. One night several visitors joined our usual crowd. It was holiday time, and it was common for people who had "graduated" to come back during tougher times. We got coffee and mulled around waiting for the meeting to start when I recognized a woman. At first I couldn't place her, but our eyes met, and I could see she recognized me too.

I walked over. "Hi! You look familiar to me. Do I look familiar to you?"

"Yes, but I can't remember how I know you."

"I'm a drug rep. I'm in pediatrics now, but I used to call on derms and plastics. Do you work in one of those offices?"

I was back to old Dawn, smiling and happy to see a friendly face, a reflex when I saw someone I knew. I momentarily forget my "new world" and approached people as if nothing happened, and then I snapped back to reality and categorized the person as either someone who knows or someone who didn't know.

"Oh, that's it. I work for Dr. Jeff. I do remember you."

Oh shit, she doesn't know.

She looked at me quizzically and with concern. I realized she was wondering why I was there. I panicked. I involuntarily jumped back as if I'd been shoved.

I don't want to talk about it. It's too early. I hadn't opened up in counseling yet and had no intention of starting that night.

"My husband died," I blurted out as I turned away.

When the session started, I was tucked in a corner, as prickly as cactus. My body language screamed, "Leave me alone!" The sharing started and circled toward the woman I knew. She said, "My husband died a few years ago, and I'm doing better now. I wasn't sure why I needed to be here tonight. I assumed it was because of the holidays, but that's not it. I know someone here whom I've just learned has suffered the same loss. She's in a lot of pain, and I hope she'll talk tonight and ease some of her pain."

Everyone looked around the room wondering whom she was referring to, and it was clear it was me. An explosion of emotions - anger, sadness, frustration, and fear - overpowered me. In seconds, my body clipped through a succession of reactions. I began to perspire, my face fell, and my lips shook. My arms crossed protectively, and the foot resting on my knee fluttered up and down at hummingbird-wing speed. Tears fell as my breathing came in gasps. Heat rushed up my chest, neck, and face, and I developed a splitting headache. All eyes were on me, and the dreaded tissue box was coming my way.

I glanced up only to look at her and whisper, "Thank you." I wasn't happy about being called out, but I knew her intentions were good, and I trusted her. I would have spit venom at anyone else.

My head fell back down as I tried to pull myself together. I blubbered like a child as I told the group that my husband died in a plane crash overseas two months earlier. I spoke of the horror of waiting three weeks for his remains to come back before we could finally have a funeral. I wiped my eyes and finished by saying, "He was exceptional." It was all I could do.

20

Third Week of November 2010

A company called BMS Global contacted me. It was in the business of disaster recovery and restoration of personal effects. The representative asked me to e-mail a list of everything Matt had with him the day of the accident. She cautioned me not to get my hopes up, because little was recovered, because of the intensity and duration of the fire.

Matt had his suitcase with him packed with uniforms, a couple changes of clothes, pajamas, and toiletries. I knew he had his laptop, iPhone, pocket camera, and a titanium watch I'd given him years before. The only thing I wanted was his wedding band. It was platinum with a thin band of eighteen-carat gold around the center of the ring. I'd had the inside engraved to read "Today my wishes come true." I prayed I'd get it back, whatever its condition. I suspected the gold had melted but assumed the platinum would have withstood the heat.

I was e-mailed a web address with a user name and password. I now had the ghastly task of scrolling through the personal effects that were recovered and claim what was my husband's. I put Ava to bed and forced myself to log on. I didn't want to see these things, objects that represented lives that were ended. I didn't want to see his watch or ring, because it made the accident real. Seeing the physical evidence would destroy my irrational hope that he somehow survived.

I looked through the pictures of random things such as eyeglass frames and a tiepin, and then there it was, his wedding band. It took my breath away, and I fell back into my chair. Tears blurred the screen. My heart jackhammered, and I hyperventilated. *Oh my God. He's really dead.*

Once I claimed his ring online, BMS contacted me to arrange delivery. I was impressed that someone would physically bring it to me rather than ship it. We agreed on Saturday, November 20, for the change of custody and release of property. I couldn't wait for the delivery person to get there; my entire body ached to hold Matt's ring. I paced in circles like a junkie waiting for a fix.

The doorbell rang and I opened the door to two women. I scanned them, looking for the ring. Neither was holding anything other than a handbag or a manila folder. They introduced themselves and said they were from BMS Global. "Are you Dawn Bell?"

"Yeah, where's the ring?" I asked tersely, ignoring all social etiquette.

"We have it, but you need to sign for it, Mrs. Bell. May we come in?" the older of the two asked calmly.

I wanted to scream "No! Give me the damn ring!" I had no interest in inviting them into my home. I preferred they just handed me the ring and leave. It was clear there was a procedure to follow, so I opened the door and led them to the kitchen table. One asked if anyone else was at home.

I shook my head as we sat down. "Just me," I said flippantly.

"Your daughter isn't here?" the other asked.

"No," I snipped, looking around and holding out my hands as if to say "Do you see her?" Even my body language was rude.

I wasn't interested in any chitchat, so I kept my answers short. I watched them watching me very closely. I was sure they were trying to evaluate the condition I was in and would be able to adjust the conversation as necessary. Deliveries of this kind were their job, and I was sure they'd seen it all. I sensed they were very kind and loving people, but I grew more and more agitated with them. I was sick of people staring at me.

They waited patiently for me to expand on my answer, but I cocked my head and moved only my gaze from one to the other. I raised my eyebrows, smirked at them, and blinked slowly and repeatedly, silently saying, "Any more stupid questions?"

They took the hint and pulled out the paperwork for my signature. I signed immediately and could tell that as I did, one of them was reaching into her handbag for the ring. I looked up at a box she placed in front of me. I dropped the pen, grabbed the box, and tore it open.

There it was, completely intact, the inscription unmarred. *How can it be?* I turned the ring over and over. I closed my hands around it and pulled it into me. I lowered my head and closed my eyes. I felt suffocated at the thought that only eleven weeks before, Matt had this ring on his finger. He was alive and his blood was flowing beneath it.

I didn't weep or cry out. I wasn't sure I was even breathing. I was in a cave devoid of sound and light. Many minutes passed before I remembered two other people were at the table. I looked up with a start, as if the women had just materialized out of nowhere. They continued to watch me and asked if I was okay.

"Yes. Thank you for bringing this to me," I whispered. I moved to stand, but they remained seated. "Is anyone coming over to be with you?"

"Actually I'm going to my friend Gina's house. She lives right there, and Ava is with her," I lied as I pointed out the bay window at the house whose yard abutted mine. The house was my friend Gina's, but I had no plan to go there. Ava was at another home.

The women were clearly uncomfortable with my being alone, but I wanted them to leave. I needed to be alone and hold Matt's ring, so I lied to them, and they left.

I wore the ring on my right thumb for about a week. It helped over the Thanksgiving holiday, but I found it sparked conversation I wasn't interested in having, so I took it off. *Why do so many people notice a ring on my thumb?* Now I wear it on special occasions or when it just feels right.

21

Thanksgiving 2010

We flew to Wisconsin for the holiday. I was on edge during the days leading up to the trip. This time I wouldn't have anyone from UPS helping me. The company response teams that assisted me on every trip prior to this one were invaluable. They handled the tickets, my ID, and luggage. When Ava was with me, they kept an eye on her and entertained her. They steered me through special security lines and circled me when we walked through the airport to the Sky Club lounges where we waited to board. When it was time to board, they escorted me protectively to the gate to board before anyone else. I didn't have to keep track of anything, speak to anyone, or make eye contact. I was able to keep my head down and follow mindlessly. The members of the response teams had all performed their jobs impeccably at every stage, but their job was finished.

This time it was only me. I had to focus and be attentive. I had to keep an eye on Ava. I had to make sure I was where I needed to be when I was supposed to be. Those details required intense concentration of which I had only a limited supply. I obsessively checked and rechecked my list of things I could not misplace: ID, tickets, handbag, luggage; ID, tickets, handbag, luggage; ID, tickets, handbag, luggage. I looked at my boarding pass for the gate number and boarding time, only to forget it seconds later. I decided to keep the pass in my hand until I was seated on the plane, because I could not commit the simple bit of information to memory.

I sensed Matt was with me on the trip, and I learned to recognize his presence through songs. Matt was a huge music fan and appreciated an eclectic array of genres. About a year before, I made this century's version of a mix tape for him. I created a playlist of about twenty-five songs on his iTunes account, all songs that reminded me of him or had special meaning to us. I titled it *Mile 22,* because in all four of the marathons he'd run, I could never spot him until that mile marker.

On this trip, four of those twenty-five songs played while I worked my way from the parking garage to my seat on the plane. The first one played while I stood at the ticketing kiosk to print our boarding passes. The second one played while we waited in the security line. We boarded the tram to take us to our concourse, and the third song from that tiny playlist wafted through the speakers. I noticed the first two songs and thought it was bizarre to hear two songs from that playlist, but hearing the third one really got my attention.

I sat and pondered the chances that three songs from a random list of twenty-five could play within minutes of each other. Of the millions upon millions of songs to queue over the satellite radio in the airport, how could I hear a third one from an incredibly short list? The songs I'd chosen for Matt's playlist were scattered over decades and genres; they weren't related enough to warrant being on the same soundtrack. Other songs played in between these three, but still, *what are the odds?*

I saw pilots throughout the airport, and they were spikes to my heart. As we boarded, the flight attendant saw Ava and asked cheerfully if she'd like to meet the pilots and get some wings. My head spun, my knees weakened, and I felt like I would collapse. Ava said "Yes," and headed toward the forward cabin. It wasn't her first time at the rodeo. I stepped out of the way for people to pass to their seats, but I kept my back to Ava and the pilots. I could not look at them. We walked to our row, and Ava chose the middle seat over the window seat. I was relieved that I could gaze through the glass and zone out.

I felt comforted by the thought of Matt reaching out to me, but feared I was verging on lunacy. The cabin door closed and the announcements started over the speakers. We were warned to turn off all electronic devices until we reached cruising altitude. I'd already put my phone on airplane mode and placed it in the side pocket of my handbag under the seat in front of me. Everyone was settling in and the flight attendants were snapping shut the overhead bins.

All of a sudden I heard the song "In Your Eyes" by Peter Gabriel. It was our song and was also on the playlist. I looked around. *Who's the fool who didn't turn off his music?*

Other people looked around too, because the volume was quite high, and we'd just been told to turn everything off. One by one, all gazes rested on me. I shot back a look of "Not me."

Ava said, "Mommy, your phone is on." I followed her pointer finger to my handbag. The side had drooped, and I saw my phone screen lit up. Peter Gabriel's album cover was displayed while his song played. I was gob smacked with disbelief. I'd just set the phone on Airplane Mode, blackened the screen, and put the device in my bag. No apps were pulled up, especially not iTunes, and I knew without a doubt that "In Your Eyes" was not the last song I'd played earlier that morning. Matt was with me at that moment, and I'll never be convinced otherwise.

I quietly sobbed the entire flight and considered our chances of crashing, but knew it was unlikely. *Would I feel fear if the plane was in a free fall? Would I scream and pray to live?* I supposed it was possible, but I didn't think so.

* * *

Ava and I spent a day with my in-laws and two nights at my parents' home. Matt's absence was heavy and surrounded us like a dense foam. My lower lip had again swollen from stress, so my sister brought me ice and hydrocortisone. It didn't help. One afternoon I lay down in an upstairs bedroom. I curled up in a cocoon of blankets and fell into a deep sleep for a couple hours. It was the most solid sleep I'd had in two and a half months, and when I opened my eyes, I felt as if I'd awoken from a month-long coma. If I were a man I would have expected to feel stubble on my face.

The night before our return flight, I joined my family in the living room. Everyone was talking and the atmosphere was pleasant. I happened to notice my brother Rich doing something absentmindedly with his hand while in conversation with my dad. For some reason, his gesture struck me as hilarious, and I burst out in hysterical laughter. No one else was laughing, but I was on a roll. All conversations stopped and everyone looked around, trying to determine what was so funny, which only wound me up more. My deep laughter felt good, and it kept bubbling through me. I didn't want it to end. I basked in the endorphin rush and smiled at the gift of hope, hope that I would get through my pain and actually feel joy again some day.

I've spoken with other people who've experienced loss, and they too could recall their first big laugh and the relief it produced, because we thought we'd never laugh again. Their stories were similar in that what produced the laughter wasn't especially funny, and no one else around them thought it was funny, yet the grievers still experienced a deep, long roar of laughter.

22

December 2010

I felt cheated, I didn't sign up for grief. It wasn't how life was supposed to go. It wasn't the path I worked so hard to be on. Matt was supposed to walk Ava down the aisle, and I was supposed to grow old with him. I grieved not just for him; I mourned the dreams our future once held.

I felt guilty for every fight we'd ever had, every mean word I'd ever said to him, even if the fights and words were a decade old and long forgiven. I couldn't recall any mean word he'd ever said to me or believe any of the fights were his fault. I learned in counseling that I was canonizing him. I was remembering only what made him wonderful but was unable to recollect his faults.

Did I love him enough? Did he know how much I loved him? Did I ever deserve him? Was I ever good enough to him or for him? No.

I couldn't picture my life without him, so I didn't know how I'd face future hurdles alone. I feared attending the next funeral. I feared I'd be alone forever, because I couldn't imagine being with anyone other than Matt. I'd developed an obsessive fear of Ava's death. If she was taken from me, I'd have no one. I woke numerous times throughout the nights to check on her, to make sure she was still breathing. I could scarcely let her out of my sight.

I wanted to scream at all of my friends who came to console me, "Shut up! Your husband could die too." I wanted someone else's husband to die. I wanted someone else to feel the pain I was feeling. I didn't want to be the only one. I scanned the obituaries because I wanted to see if someone else Matt's age died. It brought me a sick satisfaction.

In my mind I continually made comparisons to other people's tragedies. *At least Matt didn't die of disease. We did not have to watch him slowly deteriorate. At least he didn't cheat on me and leave me for someone else. At least I didn't lose him* and *my child.*

I resumed some administrative work involving Matt and my utility and financial accounts. I was a heinous version of myself on the phone with anyone in customer service. I knew at some point I would have to tell my story. I was snotty and condescending. I wanted to ruin the customer service representative's day. When I did tell the circumstances behind the call and someone offered condolences, I scoffed at them. "Hmmph. Wow…yeah…thanks for that."

I tried to order checks without his name on them, so I went online, wanting to avoid the phone. I didn't want to be evil. The website wouldn't allow me to perform the transaction electronically. A message appeared saying I must call a phone number, so I did, and I was a beast. I reasoned that the recipient deserved it, because I had to call.

I'd already updated the user names and passwords for our online accounts, but I continued to get e-mails from those same accounts sent to Matt's attention. Apparently I had overlooked a separate step. Seeing e-mails addressed to him broke my heart every time. I had to call customer service to change the account name or continue to see his name on e-mails and mail.

I was ashamed of my inability to control my behavior. I was the cruelest I had ever been in my life. I knew it was wrong but I couldn't stop. I chose my victims wisely, the way any monster would. I preyed on faceless people over the phone because they had to take my wickedness to keep my business. As long as I didn't swear or raise my voice, they wouldn't hang up. I couldn't treat my friends like that, because I'd risk losing them. I hated myself.

I was trying to work full time, take care of Ava, maintain a home, and grieve the most terrible loss I'd ever been dealt. I was in a game of Whack-a-Mole, and every time I fixed one thing, another problem popped up. I didn't know how to set the garage door to open with the buttons on my visor. I didn't know which alarm was chirping day and night, so I didn't know who to call to fix it. I didn't know home air filters had to be changed every six months, and oh, they come in different sizes?

Ava needed a recent picture for her pre-K class for a project that was sprung on me. I didn't know how to download photos from our camera onto the computer. *And then what? Upload it and somehow get it to Sam's Club?* I had cockroaches all over my garage, and I was seeing them in my house. I didn't know who sprayed our home or when pest control sprayed it last. *Did Matt spray the insecticide?* My gutters were overflowing with acorns, leaves, and twigs. *Who do I call to clean them?*

I didn't know how to reset the mini tower in my bedroom closet so I could get cell phone coverage. I didn't know how to set the sprinklers to follow the county watering restrictions. I had an issue with my Internet connection, and I didn't even know which company we subscribed to. When I finally figured it out and called, the sales representative asked which Wi-Fi system I had and where it was located. *I have no f***ing idea!*

I remember my grandfather passing away when I was a teenager. Everyone talked about how he had taken care of everything around the house and farm, and my grandmother was left not knowing how to handle things. She was born in 1907, had never gotten her driver's license, rarely bought anything, and didn't know how to write a check.

I was only fifteen at the time, but I swore I'd never be in that position when I married. I had my driver's license and I was capable of balancing our finances. I graduated with a science degree and held a job that required a high level of skill, but I had no clue how much work Matt was doing to maintain our home. I was struggling to catch up. I was slapped with the realization that I had become my grandmother.

* * *

I felt lonely and abandoned. I'd lost my best friend of sixteen years. I looked for clues everywhere, some sign that he was trying to reach out to me. I wondered if I'd ever be happy again. I lived each day feeling like a wrecking ball was sitting on my rib cage that denied me the final, merciful step to crush and end me. I felt I was doomed to a life of dragging through each day, only to wake up and scrape myself through the next one, knowing I'd never see him again in this lifetime.

One night I dreamed I was standing in front of a long mirror in a bedroom of a house that was not familiar to me. I was bent over twisting my wet hair in a towel, turban-style, to dry it. I flipped my head up, looked in the mirror, and saw Matt. His sweet face was full of concern. We stared at each other for an instant. I woke up. *No! I don't want to wake up. Put me back in the dream.* I was frustrated because I kept hoping he would appear in a dream and say something that would comfort me or give me some direction. He finally appeared and vanished before I could say anything.

My friend Sarah came to town for a work function, and we met for dinner. We used to joke about how similar I was to her husband Doug, and how alike she and Matt were. We'd laugh and say that's why we both had great marriages, and if we'd married each other's spouse, it wouldn't have worked as well.

"I'm glad he died instead of me," I admitted to her. She didn't react, just waited for me to continue.

"That doesn't mean I'm happy to be alive. What I mean is that it's so horrible to be the one left behind." My eyes welled, and it became harder to speak. "This loss is so hard and it hurts so much that I would never want Matt to go through it. Is that crazy? Is that wrong for me to say?"

"No, Dawn. That's not crazy or wrong," she answered. "You loved him so much, and it's understandable that you would never want him to feel what you're feeling."

I was flooded with relief. I needed a trusted friend to tell me I wasn't sick or evil. I knew the last twenty minutes of Matt's life had to have been filled with unimaginable fear, trying to land a plane on fire, but he died on impact. It had to be easier than what I was going through. *Thank you, Sarah.*

My mind flashed back to a conversation I had with my friend Amy Kimball years before. I told her, "If Matt died, I'd get through it, but if I died, he'd have a really tough time." I knew this experience would have been harder for Matt to endure, and I was grateful he'd never have to deal with losing his wife.

*   *   *

Children's birthday parties were surprisingly hard to attend. Matt came to every one he could, and now it was just me. As the kids played, I stood with the other mothers and fathers, prime time to get to know each other and check them out, in case their children wanted a play date with mine. I was forced to share my story with strangers. I would rather have hidden off to the side, but I didn't want Ava to see me withdrawn.

I imagined the other parents would go home after the party and at some point explain to their child that Ava's father died. Our tragedy was the perfect learning experience for their family. They could broach the subject of death, discuss what happened when someone died, and so forth.

I was angry that our loss had become a teaching tool for others. I couldn't hide our situation, but I worried how it might affect Ava as more children heard what happened. I could tolerate the sympathetic faces, the questions, and the awkwardness, but it killed me to know it could happen to Ava.

* * *

My friend Beth, who was also my hairstylist, came over one night after work. The first time she came to my house was shortly after Matt's death three months earlier. She had brought her tools and supplies and highlighted my hair in my bathroom. She then offered to fly up to Wisconsin to repeat the process before Matt's funeral. I broke down sobbing, and she wrapped her arms around me and held me until I stopped. She's a true friend.

On that December night she returned after a fourteen-hour workday on her feet and still had a forty-five-minute drive home ahead of her. She arrived with presents for Ava, all kinds of hair things; spray glitter and coloring, clip-in feathers, barrettes, and more. She also brought bottles of nail polish and stick-on decorations. My girlie-girl was beyond excited. *Thank you, Beth.*

* * *

My friend Carrie invited us over to decorate home-baked gingerbread houses. She has a son Ava's age and another boy two years younger. The three of them were thrilled and I was grateful Ava was entertained with a project she enjoyed. Carrie provided frosting, candies, chocolate chips, and sprinkles to make yummy houses. I watched the children giggling as they decorated, and I sadly acknowledged that I never would have had the energy or ambition to put together such a project for Ava at home. *Thank you, Carrie.*

* * *

Christmas shopping was difficult because I kept seeing things I'd have loved to buy for Matt. That year I limited all purchases to one national toy store. My strategy allowed me to stay out of the mall to avoid seeing menswear and other items Matt would have liked as gifts.

I needed to decorate the house, but it was a daunting task because Christmas was always Matt's and my favorite holiday. I started with the tree, because if I finished only one thing, at least the tree would be up. It was a fake one that came in three sections. It was pre-wired with a string of little white lights and another string with sockets for colored light bulbs. I made the mistake of putting the middle section of the tree in the tree stand rather than the lower section. I pulled down all of the branches and fanned them out carefully. I reached back into the box and realized my mistake when I unpacked the true bottom section of the tree. *Brilliant.*

Erecting the tree took me numerous attempts. I needed to connect the cords to the correct lights on each section. I grew more irritated by the minute and fantasized about dousing the whole mess with gas and starting a fire. I cursed far too many times, considering the reason for the season. After hours of frustration, I finally aligned the cords so all three sections of white lights turned on when I stepped on the switch and all three sections of colored lights came on when I stepped on another switch.

Ava was handing me colored lights and accidentally dropped a few. I screamed at her, not quite the festive atmosphere recounting Jesus's birth that we'd had in the past. I saw hurt and sadness flash across her face a second before she looked down at her hands. I was racked with self-hatred and shame.

"I'll be right back," I said as I escaped to my dark bedroom. I paced in circles to release a mountain of emotions. I cried, said a prayer over and over, and begged for help from God, Matt, and anybody looking over us. I kept circling, reminding myself of all the great Christmases I'd experienced in the past. I vowed not to let my rage and exasperation define this year.

I began to calm down, my pacing and breathing slowed, and I felt the tension softening in my neck. I stopped moving, took three deep breaths, and returned to Ava. In my absence she had continued to decorate by putting Matt's childhood ornaments on the few branches she could reach. The scene was heartbreaking. I had never despised myself more in my entire life.

I returned to my room. I stopped my fall against the wall with my forehead and hands and cried. *Why, Why, Why? Why is Matt dead, when child molesters live? Why would you take him? What could possibly be the lesson? What good can come of his death? Tell me! Make me understand why.*

I pulled myself together a second time and returned to Ava. I moved an ottoman next to her and sat. I held out my hands, inviting her to sit on my lap. She did, and I pulled her close to me and hugged her like it was the first time.

"I'm so sorry I yelled at you, Ava. It wasn't your fault. Nothing was your fault. Mommy's just really sad and really angry because Daddy isn't here. I'm not good at putting up trees and stuff, and that makes me angry too."

"It's okay, Momma."

"Thanks, sweetie. I'll be nice now, I promise. I should never have yelled at you. Do you want to hear about my first Christmas with Daddy?"

"Yeah!"

"Okay. Well, back then we lived in Wisconsin, and one day he bought a real pine tree, pulled it up all the stairs to our apartment, and sprayed it with white, sticky stuff so it looked like it had snow all over it."

"Really? Did it look like snow?"

"Yes, it did. When I came home from work it was all decorated, except for one ornament he had in his hand. It was a beautiful glass one that said 'Our First Christmas 1996,' and he gave it to me to put on the tree. We were married four months before that, so it was our first Christmas together as husband and wife. It's still here somewhere. We'll find it."

"Did you put it on the tree?"

I chuckled. "Well, of course I did! And then your daddy let me open a present early. He always did that, because he couldn't wait until Christmas morning. He loved Christmas as much as any kid, even though he was all grown up."

"What was the present?"

"It was beautiful silk pajamas. They were red and had a separate top and bottom, like some of your pajamas. I loved them. I'd never had silk pajamas, and you know what? I brought them with me to wear in the hospital when you were born, and I still have them"

"Can I see?" She squealed with delight and her eyes widened.

I took her hand and brought her into my room to show her my silk pajamas. She touched them with the gentleness she would touch a baby rabbit.

"Your dad made Christmas special every year, Ava. He'd wrap everything as beautifully as you would see in a magazine. When he was a little boy, he couldn't wait to open his presents, so he would sneak down in the night, open them, and then wrap them back up."

"Really? Did Santa know?" she asked with the innocence and wonder of any four-year-old.

"Well, I'm sure he knew, but your father opened only the presents from his mom and dad. The presents from Santa didn't come until Christmas Eve, and your daddy didn't open them until he was supposed to."

We put on some Christmas music and finished decorating the tree. I ended up putting out almost all the holiday decorations in the days following. The more I did, the better I felt. But I never sent out Christmas cards that year. I couldn't bear to sign them without his name.

* * *

I caught a cold about a week before Christmas and lost my voice. It was frustrating, because I was on holiday break from work and had a list of business and personal calls to make. I spun myself into a tizzy trying to get everything done. I finally threw in the towel, quit trying to force a sentence beyond a whisper, and put away my To Do list. I literally couldn't talk to anybody and instead texted messages to those who reached out to me. Ultimately, though, I lay around, drank hot tea, and sipped broth for three days. The only list I tackled was the one with books I wanted to read. My cat curled up around me as I read, and the only sound I heard for hours on end was his purring. It was glorious, and I'm thankful for what can only have been a Christmas gift. Silence truly is golden, both internally and externally.

Christmas fell on a Saturday in 2010, so we flew up to my brother Rich's on Friday and stayed until Monday. Most of it's a blur, but we had a nice time, and I was happy to see Ava play the whole weekend with her cousins. I had wanted to stay in Florida, but everyone told me to get out of the house for the holidays, so I did. It was wise advice I would recommend to other grievers.

23

January 2011

I joined some friends for dinner at my favorite restaurant on the night of New Year's Day. I felt a sense of relief that 2010 was over. Our waiter was Chinese, and I asked him what year 2011 was on the Chinese calendar. He answered it would be the year of the rabbit, but the Chinese year would not turn over until the next month, on February 3. The rabbit celebrated people who enjoyed being surrounded by family and friends. He added that it represented hope. *How ironic, because I feel hopeless.*

I had to fly to Dallas to attend a national meeting for a week. My brother Rich flew down with one of his daughters to take care of the girls, the cats, and the house while I'd be away. I was incredibly anxious. I didn't want to go to the meeting and face everyone. I feared the awkwardness I knew was coming.

More than 400 sales representatives were present as well as district managers and many people from the home office. In the hallways walking to the general sessions or to meals, I felt people watching me. I knew they were whispering to one another, "That's her. That's the girl whose husband died."

I had a glimmer of what it might be like to be a celebrity. People stared at me, scrutinizing every facial expression and word I said. I had to keep up appearances by being groomed and dressed appropriately at all times. I had to keep my head up and pay attention to everything around me. I had to show the appropriate reaction or no reaction. I ached for anonymity, so that people would quit watching me.

The loneliness I felt was devastating. It was hard to look at other couples, but I couldn't seem to look away from them. I wondered if they were happy and watched how they interacted. I wondered if they appreciated each other, if they thought about how lucky they were. I wondered if a widow ever observed Matt and me the same way.

I had new boundaries as a young widow. I sensed women watching me when I talked with their husbands, men I commonly spoke with months earlier. Many times a wife would cross the room to join in the conversation I was having with her husband. One time a woman placed herself physically between her husband and me at a gathering, and it was quite awkward. It was unfortunate, because I missed the company of men. I'd always had male friends, but now I stayed away from them.

I was angry for much of January. Matt's birthday was January 11, and I couldn't believe a man like him was not allowed to turn thirty-nine. I dwelled on thoughts of all the horrible, selfish, and cruel people still alive and thriving in the world. It fueled my anger, and I bounced around like a jumble of barbed wire, ready to tear whomever I came into contact with to shreds.

I was surprised at how angry and mean I could still be. I was shocked by how my body was reacting to the stress and trauma I was going through, and admittedly, I was intrigued. I've always been in awe of how our bodies work, which is what led me to pursue a science degree. We have an amazing inner system of checks and balances, and our bodies have one primary goal: stay alive by any means necessary. When I was pregnant with Ava, I was fascinated as I watched and felt my body change throughout the nine months. After losing Matt, I was equally as interested in my voluntary, involuntary, physical, and mental reactions to grief.

I turned to journaling after Matt's death to bring me comfort. I wrote all my observations and thoughts. I looked for books that would help me with what I was going through, but the only ones I could find were textbooks that contained a chapter describing the body in trauma. I read a couple books by women who had lost their husbands, but I couldn't find one that resonated with me. I wanted someone to tell me what coursed through her head when she was angry, not just that she was angry. I wanted someone to validate my feelings and tell me I wasn't crazy. I kicked around the idea of writing my own book someday about this time in my life. *What would I title it?*

I lay awake in bed one evening wound up from a day of having to fill out more forms relating to Matt's death. They all started with a box or line where I was supposed to write my name. Underneath that line was written: Spouse of the Deceased. *Huh? How about that?* I hissed to myself, *I guess that's my new title.* A light bulb went on in my head. My title, that's my new title. I determined that if I did write a book, I would call it *Wife of the Deceased.*

* * *

I arrived at my doctor's appointment, and since it was a new year, I needed to fill out my insurance information again. The form asked my status with the options: married, single, divorced, widowed. My stomach knotted. I considered checking single, but I didn't want to discount our marriage. I knew widow was the right descriptor, so I checked the box. It seemed final on this paper, accepted, but not to me.

The nurse called me back, and I followed her to the scale. She wrote my weight in the chart and paged back to the notes from my visit six months earlier. I had been twenty-eight pounds heavier and within my ideal weight range in August.

She looked concerned. "You've lost some weight, huh?"

"Yep," I said as I stepped down. Deep breath. "My husband died in September. I'm doing the best I can."

"I'm so sorry Dawn...I didn't know. You're thin for your height. You're five feet five, right?"

"Umm, yeah," I lied, but my face gave me away. I never was good at lying. I'm actually five feet seven, but my weight wouldn't be such a concern if I were a couple inches shorter. I was tired of the "you need to eat" talks.

She had me step back on the scale and she raised the measuring stick. "You're five feet seven," she said and our eyes met. We both knew I lied, but nothing more was said. She led me into the lab room.

A couple minutes later my doctor knocked and poked his head in. He gently asked me how I was doing.

Tears welled, and I told him I was as good as could be expected. "I know I've lost some weight, but I'm eating as much as I can. If I eat a lot or anything greasy, it hurts my stomach and I end up in the bathroom. I eat toast for breakfast, and every night I eat a spinach, tomato, avocado, and mozzarella salad. I put lots of olive oil on it too. I'm not gaining weight, but I've stopped losing it, and I've been at this weight for about a month."

"Okay, Dawn. Try to add smoothies or chocolate milk too. I'm going to send you to the lab to get your blood work. Come back next week, and we'll go over the results. Are you sleeping well?"

"No. I keep replaying the last minutes of his life and I..."I started crying and could not continue.

He scribbled a prescription for a sleep aid and handed it to me. He asked how Ava was doing and encouraged me to seek counseling for both of us if I hadn't already. I walked out and threw the prescription away; I'd already tried it and the results were minimal. Only a coma would stop my sleep deprivation.

A week later my blood work revealed that all my levels were fine and I was very healthy. All the spinach and avocados gave me an excellent iron level. The nurse who called me with the results urged me to try to eat more and put on at least five more pounds. She lectured me that being underweight could affect my immune system and could result in my nutritional reserves being minimized. *Would you care as much if I'd gained the same amount of weight instead of lost it?*

My weight loss exposed me to a shocking number of unsolicited comments. Most were out of concern, but some of them were snippy and unkind, with an element of jealousy. If people knew the circumstances that caused my weight loss, no one would have been jealous. Criticism was thrown at me with the insinuation that I had an eating disorder or that there was something wrong with me and I was too stupid to know it. I was blindsided by strangers' comments, because I kept forgetting I was thin. I assumed they were talking to someone else, and by the time I realized the comment was directed at me, it was too late to retort.

I forced myself not to scream, "My husband died! I can't eat! Got anything else to say?"

My clothes didn't fit anymore, so I had to take time and money to buy new sizes. I had no idea when I had lost the weight, and I suspected I'd gain it back eventually. I assumed my shopping spree would all be in vain. I was already thinking of whom I would give the clothes to when the weight returned.

I brought clothes one size smaller than my usual into the dressing room. I was horrified to see my reflection. The clothes hung on me like I was a child in my older sister's clothes. The fitting room attendant saw me in the three-way mirror and said, "That's falling off you, girl. Eat a French fry!"

I knew she meant her comment as a compliment, but it crushed me. I was actually a bit frightened. I felt as if I were dressing an unfamiliar body and couldn't make the clothes work, like I'd been abducted by aliens and returned with a different body. I thought of Lisbeth Salander, Stieg Larsson's title character in his Millenium book series. She was incredibly thin and obviously annoyed with the weight comments constantly thrown at her. Her immediate and rehearsed defense was something to the effect of "I have a metabolic disorder that doesn't allow me to gain weight." *I may borrow that.*

* * *

I brought my car in to be cleaned, and when I got back in it, I noticed the seat had been moved to aid in vacuuming. My programmed seat position was the number-one button, and Matt's was the number-two button. Even though the car was his, he put me as number one, another glaring example of how Matt always put me first. I accidentally pressed the number-two button and felt the seat moving back to accommodate his long legs. I burst into tears.

* * *

I pulled into Ava's school to pick her up. I idled behind a line of parents doing the same thing. I noticed all the decals on their back windows, the ones with the stick figure outlines to represent the father, mother, and kids. Some even had animals. I felt anger and envy of their complete families. I wanted to jump out of my car, rip all the decals off, and crumple them in front of the drivers. I just looked away, though. I immediately thought of something to be grateful for and acknowledged my relief at never having put the decals on my car in the first place. I couldn't imagine having to remove the father.

Even something as silly as working a crossword puzzle could bring me hours of sadness. I used to love Sunday mornings curled up next to Matt. He'd read the paper while I worked the crossword puzzle. When a clue asked about the Greek alphabet or a country's currency, I'd ask Matt. If I read a clue on one of those topics, I was reminded that I could never ask him a question again.

I'd expected the big things to hurt, such as holidays, birthdays, telling people for the first time, and so forth. I learned that my body alerted me physically, to ready me for stressors. On the days leading up to special occasions, my adrenaline began to race. My skin reacted with eczematous outbreaks, I'd suffer a headache that wouldn't go away, and I was edgy. In time, I could recognize the uncomfortable changes, and they helped me prepare for trying times.

I was ambushed by the small stuff, however, things such as adjusting the car seat, seeing the window decals, smelling Matt's cologne on another man passing by me, getting mail and e-mail to Matt's attention, hearing songs that held a special meaning to us, and picking up my dry cleaning that included something of his I was not expecting.

The mounds, not the mountains, are what I learned to be wary of. The little stuff felt like a sledgehammer to my head. It threw me into a whirlpool of emotions: anger, sadness, fear, self-pity, and frustration. I slowly spiraled down toward the deep abyss of depression. If you have ever been in the pits of depression and escaped, you will do anything to keep from returning. I was terrified as I sensed its approach. Darkness. Absolute despair. I was desperate, fighting with everything I had, to stop the horrifying descent. I was in thick, black quicksand, and it was pulling me down, deeper and deeper into the pit of hopelessness. I felt the cold and darkness consume me like an evil serpent. Once it took control, the light would extinguish. I've never known a more wretched place, and I swear hell could not be worse. I'd reach for every coping mechanism I had to stay above ground, but nothing I possessed was strong enough. I couldn't fight a giant demon with a toothpick.

Falling into depression feels similar to what I imagine being in an avalanche feels like. I was spun around and around countless times, boring deeper and deeper. When the tumbling finally ended, I did not know which way was up. In each period of depression, I didn't know if I had the strength to or if I even wanted to exert the strength to pull myself out. It seemed easier to do nothing and just wait for death.

The bouts of deep depression occurred without warning. They lasted three to five days, and when I finally came out, I felt I'd survived a bombing. I'd check to see that my body was still intact and able to function. A feeling of cautious elation followed. *Whew! I made it.*

Each time, I wanted to believe I was through the worst and the crushing pain would never return, but it did return.

I fell in and out of depression numerous times the first year. Our bodies are programmed to self-preservation, so I knew I was given the deepest grief in pieces, like a saline drip, because I could not handle it all at once. As the months passed, the bouts were fewer and further in between. I learned I could come out of such depths a little more quickly when I stopped fighting it. I no longer pretended it wasn't happening or pushed myself or carried on business as usual. I acknowledged it. I slowed down and waited for the depression to run its course.

In an uncommon move, I put me first, an unnatural thing to do when you're a mother, but I knew I had to do it. I couldn't help Ava if I didn't heal. I couldn't speed through the process, or it would affect every relationship I had at present and in the future. I put myself first for Ava and me.

Winston Churchill said, "When you're going through hell, keep on going," and that's exactly what I did. I accepted that the process would be long. I reminded myself that death has been occurring since the beginning of time, and if that many people could survive a loss, so could I. I gave myself permission to grieve rather than deny it. A younger me would have ignored it. Ten years earlier, my ego would have convinced me that I was stronger than the average person and I could deal with everything better than most. I am not extraordinary, though. I'm human, and I chose to cut myself some slack.

In her 1969 book *On Death and Dying*, Elisabeth Kübler-Ross first proposed the five stages of loss and grief:

(1) denial and isolation, (2) anger, (3) bargaining, (4) depression, and (5) acceptance. At its origination it was believed that we progressed through each stage in order and only once. Now it's understood we cycle through the stages over and over and in no particular order. I observed the chaotic order and repetition to be true in my grieving process. Sometimes I skipped a step or two and spent more time with my favorites, anger and depression.

The only reason I achieved any progress was because I faced my grief head on. I didn't deny it, ignore it, or minimize it. I didn't numb it with pills or excessive alcohol. I had amazing friends who allowed me to express my feelings. They listened without judgment countless times and were essential to my recovery.

24

February 2011

On Matt's and my first Valentine's Day together in 1995, I came home to find the kitchen table moved into the living room. Matt set the table beautifully with china and crystal he'd borrowed from his mother. A vase of beautiful red roses became the centerpiece. The only light in the room shone from candles on the table and those he'd set up around the room. He'd blown up balloons with a silver imprint saying I Love You and taped them randomly to the walls. The balloons were clear but for the imprint, so in the candlelight, I could see only the words I Love You floating around the room. The scene was breathtaking.

He always spoiled me and swore it wouldn't end when we married. He kept that promise. He never once forgot a birthday, anniversary, or special day. He also bought me cards or flowers for no reason at all, because he said there weren't enough designated days to do it. One time he bought me a funny apology card because I'd dreamed he was mean to me.

After dating for seven months, he sent me flowers at work with a card that read, "Bet you didn't think I'd remember Sweetest Day!" I remember thinking, *What's Sweetest Day?*

He always planned unique and enjoyable things to do. One night we had a vanilla date. Our dinner consisted of vanilla ice cream with vanilla pudding and vanilla Coke. We ate on the sofa and watched Vanilla Sky.

Matt had a big personality and crazy sense of humor. We had many inside jokes and constantly laughed with and at each other. He put up with my character flaw that caused me to laugh every time someone hurt himself; no broken bones or bloodshed, but things like stubbing a toe or tripping over something. He was quite accident prone, and it put me in stitches. I tried my best to hold my laughter until I scooted out of earshot so he wouldn't get angry with me. I'd hear him yelling behind me, "What is wrong with you?"

Once Matt bought a set of champagne glasses he was quite proud of. He surprised me with dinner and told me all he'd learned about crystal and the great quality of the glassware. He rambled on, but I didn't mind; he had an appreciation for fine quality. He opened the champagne bottle in our tiny kitchen and the cork blew out of the bottle, bounced off two walls, hit his glass, and broke it. I burst out in uncontrollable laughter. I thought the incident was funny because we both watched the cork like cats watching a squirrel. He didn't think it was funny at all, and I apologized for years for that one.

He in turn loved to put me on the spot in awkward situations. One time I needed to buy clothes for work but was frustrated because I'd put on a few pounds and my regular size was snug. He held up a pair of wool pants and said, "How about these? What's your size?"

Knowing the thicker wool would add to my girth, I shot back, "Oh, I'm a size Fat."

Matt didn't skip a beat and walked right up to a sales clerk with the pants and said, "My girlfriend said she'd like these in a Fat. Do you have that size?"

The clerk walked over to me and offered to tell me about their different sizing for different shapes. He was already laughing on his way out the door. He walked out quickly because he'd done something similar before, and I'd given a sad face to the clerk and said, "My boyfriend said he'd love me more if I were thinner."

We believed we could accomplish anything as long as we did it together. We were each other's biggest fan and defined ourselves as a team. On our six-year anniversary, I was going to get matching T-shirts with TEAM BELL screen-printed on the sleeve. I never did. I saw something else that seemed more fitting. I wish I had bought them.

As time went on, we grew closer and closer. In our thirties, we rarely fought. If we did, it usually ended in laughter, because we didn't want to fight with our best friend, and the argument was usually trivial anyway. After years of marriage, people seeing us for the first time would ask if we were newlyweds. A friend once said, "I bet you guys never fight." We didn't much at that time, but we definitely did in our twenties.

I knew I was not easy to live with in our early years together. I put Matt through hell. I always wanted my way and I never fought fair. I'd scream and swear and bring up earlier fights that were supposed to have been forgiven. I'd then ignore him. *Quite a catch, wasn't I?* I did some inconsiderate and self-serving things, and in the fight that followed, I'd all but dare him to leave me. I treated him like he was replaceable, when deep down I knew he wasn't. My greatest fear was that he would leave me, but my pride forbade me to tell him that. I wouldn't even cry in front of him, because I refused to show vulnerability. As great as he was, I still kept a protective wall between us for years.

He wasn't perfect either, though, and he did some thoughtless things to me. Initially he defended himself, but he'd later apologize and swear never to do it again. He rarely made the same mistake twice. He had a deep respect for me and reasoned that if I was angry or hurt, it must be justified.

It sounds like a Lifetime movie, but I never thought I deserved him. He was an attractive, hilarious, intelligent, well-dressed, pre-med major in the coolest fraternity on campus. Many girls I deemed more suitable for him wanted to date him. I believed it was just a matter of time before he cheated on me or left me for someone better, but he never did.

I was uncomfortable with myself at that time in my life. I had bad hair and outdated clothes, and I clearly lacked self-confidence unless I was around people I knew. He couldn't see it. He thought I hung the moon.

We got the worst of each other in our twenties, and we were rewarded with the best of each other in our thirties.

* * *

Ava and I had attended counseling at New Hope twice by this time. I shared with others that I was surprised I was still doing stupid things. Ava and I love live theater, so in an attempt to have some fun, I took her to a nearby production of *Steel Magnolias*. Steel Magnolias! Did I forget how the story ends or something? What was I thinking?

It didn't even occur to me how it ended until we were in our seats and the play started. We left after the third act to avoid Shelby's death scene.

* * *

On February 11, Ava's pre-K class was holding a Valentine's Day dance and all parents were invited to join. The boys had practiced asking the girls to dance and the girls had practiced accepting. The highlight of the party was the couples dance, followed by cake and ice cream.

I wasn't going to go. Even though I was working in an area just north of the school, I didn't want to face everyone. I told myself that it wasn't a big deal and Ava wouldn't mind anyway.

A half hour before the dance started, I was leaving one pediatric office and planned to go straight to the next one. I wasn't sure of the quickest route, so I put the next office's address in my Garmin GPS and got on my way. I knew the area fairly well and assumed it would be a quick drive within the city limits, but an odd thing happened.

As I approached the ramp to the road that would take me away from the city and toward the interstate, my Garmin directed me to take the ramp. *This can't be right; the next office is in the city,* but I didn't trust my compromised brain to get me where I needed to go, so I followed the Garmin direction.

I drove out of the city and toward the interstate. My Garmin froze except for a flashing red question mark and the word *recalculating*. It was taking its sweet time to recalculate, so I turned onto the interstate and kept driving. By the time it recalculated, I'd given up on getting to that office. I mentally ran through the list of other doctors I could see instead, when I realized I was near the exit by my daughter's preschool. *I wonder what Ava's doing right now. Isn't that dance today? Wait! That dance starts in ten minutes!*

I reeled my car toward the exit and raced in to the party a minute before it started. I saw my daughter crying in the arms of one of her teachers. I bee-lined to her and asked her what was wrong. Ava turned to me with the most precious and widest smile and said, "Momma, you're here!" and jumped into my arms. I looked at the teacher with confusion.

She said, "Ava really wanted you here today. She was sad that you wouldn't be coming. We're glad you made it."

I cannot even describe how happy I was to be at my daughter's event. I had no idea it meant so much to Ava. Throughout the party she kept glancing my way to make sure I was still there. I felt guilty and promised never to miss another event at her school.

One month later I was working in the same city just north of Ava's school again. I left the exact same office as the previous time, needing to proceed to the second office I'd missed the previous month. On my Garmin I pulled up the address for the second office and tapped Go. I approached the ramp that I was incorrectly directed to take the previous time. *Are you going to tell me to take the ramp out to the interstate again?* It didn't. Instead, the Garmin guided me to go straight, so I did. It brought me directly to the second office, which was only a half mile up on the right. *Was that you, Matt?*

* * *

My birthday is at the end of February, and that year, I was turning forty. I was delighted by the amount of attention I was given from my family and friends who visited throughout the month. My brother Ashley, my sister Chris, and their families flew down from Wisconsin. My brother Rich and his daughter were just down from Minnesota the month before. My brother David and his family were not far from me and stayed in close touch. They all helped me out with things around the house that needed repair or maintenance.

My friend Renee flew down from Cincinnati for a weekend. I was happy to see her because I adore her, and I also wanted her thoughts on how Ava was doing. Renee lost her father when she was almost the exact age as Ava. Although Renee wasn't academically trained in grief counseling, she had been a volunteer at loss-counseling centers.

Renee walked on the beach with Ava one afternoon and observed her over the weekend. She told me later, "Ava seems to be coping pretty well, but she closes down when I ask about Matt. That's normal, though, because she doesn't know me well. Is she still open with you?"

"Yes, we talk quite a bit about it. Not every day anymore, but several times a week. It usually happens on the way home from New Hope. Her questions hit me in the back of the head like tennis balls fired out of a practice machine. I know she gets it that he's dead, but she seems to think he may come back or that God will send him back when he's all better. It's especially hard because his schedule was to fly two weeks and be home two weeks. At first *I* thought he'd come through the door any minute from his last trip. It's got to be even harder for a four-year-old to process."

"This is common in children ages four to six. They can't understand death as being finite, so they think the person will come back. A four-year old will also have a hard time verbalizing everything. I know she'll be five next month, but she doesn't know the language to accurately describe her feelings. Keep encouraging her to talk, because her grief is substantial. For every feeling and thought she has, tell her it's normal and okay. If you share the same feeling or thought, tell her."

"I do, and I definitely don't hide my tears from her. Sometimes she rolls her eyes and seems annoyed if I cry."

"She likely wants all the commotion to be over with, and it probably scares her to see you sad, but keep doing it. Her grief will be just as individual as yours is."

Thank you, Renee.

* * *

Four good friends took me out for dinner to celebrate my birthday. Leading up to this benchmark year, I didn't have the attitude I would've had six months earlier. Instead of being gloomy about my age, my revised attitude was that I *got* to be forty. Not everyone gets to.

We drove to my favorite Irish pub to get fish and chips and a couple pints, which was all I wanted. I had asked my friends not to alert the waiter or the band that it was my birthday. I didn't want the attention, and I couldn't shake the sadness that Matt wasn't with me.

The band was playing great Irish jigs, and the place was packed. I was enjoying myself and grateful for my wonderful friends. Suddenly the music stopped and I heard the lead singer say, "I hear we've got a birthday in the house tonight."

I froze. My friends all looked at me, and I could tell by their faces they had not said a word about my birthday. My heart pace picked up as I slowly turned my back to the band. The table next to us erupted in cheers and applause. An older gentleman stood up with a huge smile and put on a birthday hat. "I'm eight-five today," he said with triumph.

We all clapped and I breathed a sigh of relief. I gazed at the man full of joy, and all I could think was, *Please, God, don't make me live another forty-five years.*

* * *

The New York insurance company I'd been squab-bling with since November for the last of Matt's insurance checks sent a check. I was confused on how to invest it and whether or not I should pay off my mortgage. A couple close friends recommended I talk to a financial advisor, and they both referred me to Todd Woodard at Mosaic Wealth Management. He was kind and explained everything in layman's terms, because the world of finance was new to me. He helped me list my assets and debts; create a budget of monthly, quarterly, semi-annual, and annual bills; and determine how much I needed to maintain my lifestyle. He invested my insurance benefits conservatively to last my lifetime, provided I stayed on a sensible budget, which enabled me to quit my job.

As much as I loved my position at Galderma Laboratories, I was ecstatic to be able to be home and focus on Ava. I was at the end of my rope in grief, trying to be a mother to Ava, working full-time, and maintaining our home. I decided I would finish out the quarter and submit my resignation at the end of March.

25

March 2011

Ava and I attended a New Hope counseling session in early March. A young mother of two shared that she had just passed the one-year anniversary of her husband's death. I was insanely jealous and felt anger bubbling inside me. She had hit all her firsts, and I'd just met the six-month point. I was eager to fast-forward through my grief, even though I knew it was not possible. I wanted the dark cloud shadowing every area of my life to blow away.

Another woman in her late thirties talked about the loss of her father. I wanted to scream at her, "Shut up! You lost your father? Big f***ing deal; he lived a long life. Why don't you give up your seat to someone who needs it?" Yes, Evil Dawn had resurfaced. Even fellow grievers weren't spared.

I learned a few new vocabulary words at New Hope: integration, fragmentation, and escapism. Integration is when your mind works to restore itself to being whole versus fragmented. Fragmentation is an effect of our defense mechanisms when dealing with grief or other tragic events. My understanding was that integration represented a level of acceptance of the death on the griever's part. During integration, grievers make changes such as reorganizing the bedroom or giving away clothes and other possessions of the deceased. I hadn't done those things yet. My home was still in suspended animation. Of course I had nothing of Matt's to trip over or clean. He was meticulous, with a Type A personality. Everything was in its place, always, especially before he left on a trip. The last thing Matt ever wanted was for me to pick up after him.

Escapism is a tendency to seek distraction and relief from unpleasant realities by mentally escaping from one's own world. People can escape into books, movies, hobbies, exercise, wrapping themselves up in someone else's life, or focusing only on their own past before the death. The only escape that brought me any relief was exercise; the other options weren't helpful to me. If I imagined seeing Matt again, it wasn't comforting at all. It hurt worse, because I had to face the truth again. Other distractions backfired. When I attempted to get lost in a book, inevitably I was reminded of Matt or a memory of us.

I tried to watch a movie and chose *Wall Street 2*. I thought it would be safe, because although there was a love interest between the main character and Gordon Gecco's daughter, it wasn't central to the movie. I walked into the dark theater and was immediately saddened that Matt was not there to take my hand. He used to automatically reach for my hand inside a dark room, because he knew I became temporarily blinded. My eyes respond slower than normal when I go from normal lighting to extreme darkness or bright light. Alone, I had to feel my way along the seats.

The movie began, and in an early scene the main character is gifting Asian businessmen with an expensive bottle of scotch. The point was to show his cultural awareness and business acumen, but all it did was break my heart. The gift wasn't just any scotch; it was Matt's favorite, Johnny Walker Blue.

* * *

My parents visited and were surprised to learn I now attended church every Sunday. I also finished the course to become a member at Saint Andrew's Chapel. The Welcoming Ceremony for new members would commence the next month, and I was looking forward to it.

I hadn't been to church in about twenty years, basically since I'd left home. Under my parents' roof, we children were required to go every week, even if we were ill. Once I moved out on my own, I stopped going. I was frustrated with religion. It felt stern and inflexible. It made me feel that being human was something to be ashamed of, because we were such sinful beasts with minimal hope for redemption. The church as a building hadn't felt warm or loving to me; it felt accusatory and damning.

I saw what I thought to be hypocrisy in the behavior of many churchgoers. Their Sunday morning façade disappeared as the day and week wore on. The doctrine insinuated that only good people went to church, but I knew many families that never attended and were kind, good people. I couldn't believe that God would condemn them to eternal damnation for not going to church. I thought it was crazy for any religion to preach its believers were the chosen; that only its members would be allowed into heaven. I couldn't believe that nonsense.

In a search for answers, I took a religious studies course in college and was fascinated by all the different beliefs. I read many books full of ideas I'd never heard of. I settled on the creed that God was within all of us. No religion, culture, race, sexual orientation, or gender was extra special. We all came from God, and we would all return to him. We were the only creatures given a conscience, and we needed to follow it. Do what we knew to be right. If in doubt, we should follow the Golden Rule: treat others as you yourself would like to be treated.

When I prayed or asked God for guidance with a problem, I felt comforted. I felt that someone had my back and loved me, no matter what. For twenty years I didn't return to my church or seek another, because I enjoyed what felt like religious freedom. I was happy to follow my conscience and keep a quiet, personal relationship with God. It worked for me for a long time.

But then Matt died and my world imploded. I could not come through it without help, without God's help. I needed the discipline of weekly worship. I needed someone to read the Bible aloud and remind me of how much God loves us. I found those things at Saint Andrew's Chapel. Ava and I were welcomed with open arms.

I've come to realize that my absence from the church stunted my spiritual growth. I had myself convinced I could worship individually, but I wasn't reading the Bible, nor did I have specific time set aside to focus on my faith.

I was lazy and undisciplined. I was even annoyed by people who referenced the Bible or spoke of God in a conversation with me. I always thought they should keep their religious beliefs to themselves. I did.

My friend Kristy shared with me a sermon she'd heard that gave me some perspective. My relationship with God was little more than my relationship with a celebrity. I might know of Angelina Jolie, for example. I know her father is Jon Voigt and she has a long-standing relationship with Brad Pitt. I know they have children; some biological, some adopted. I can tell you some movies she's been in and repeat things she's said in interviews. I can also Google her and tell you more things, as though I know her, but I don't know her. I've never spoken to her. I've never met her or been invited to her child's birthday party. I don't know her favorite color, her favorite meal, or what memory always makes her smile. I don't know her. And I didn't know God either.

Many people treat their faith the same way, at a distance. They believe in God and pray here and there and try to be good people every day. They think, "I'm a spiritual person," but don't attend church except for the major holidays, if at all. Many people don't read or speak of the Bible. Maybe that is enough for them, but it wasn't for me, not after Matt died.

Some people may not find a church that preaches everything they agree with, but that's okay. Honestly, they probably never will. I would encourage them to go anyway and hear God's words. It will keep them mindful of their purpose. I see people in church who send text messages during services, play word puzzles, or continually check their watches because there's someplace they need to be. Instead of looking at them and thinking they are prime examples of why not to go to church, I now look at them and am glad they're at least attending. I'm grateful they will have their faith to turn to in the event of a tragedy, even if their faith is not a priority to them today.

I know people with cold hearts will continue to attend church; they are the hypocrites who drop the façade as the Sunday or week wears on. Instead of judging as I once so self-righteously did, I commend them for making the effort to walk through the doors on Sunday morning. I hope that one sermon, one day, will change their hearts. Who was the real hypocrite all along? I was, judging everybody else.

A few months after I wrote this chapter, an interesting thing happened. One of our pastors gave a sermon on the top objections people have to attending church. He focused on the objection that only hypocrites go. I thought he was talking right to me. He said that people are not hypocrites if they attend church yet continue to sin, because we all continue to sin. They are hypocrites only if they say they do not sin, but then sin.

* * *

Ava's fifth birthday was coming at the end of the month. I was sad for her that Matt was not here. I regretted that she was stuck with me instead of him, and I wondered if she felt the same. He always put her first and was patient and playful with her. Even if he was exhausted after coming home from a long trip and plagued with jet lag, he dug deep to find energy to play with her.

I hired the Fun Bus to come to her school because her birthday was on a weekday. The bus was painted crazy colors, and all the seats had all been removed. The interior had been transformed into a jungle gym and obstacle course for the kids. They played games, sang songs, and slid down the slide out the back emergency door. Ava had a great time and enjoyed cake and ice cream afterward in the cafeteria.

When we went home she was elated to find every present on her birthday wish list. Such extravagance was not standard operating procedure for me, but that year, I didn't care. She was getting spoiled.

I remembered my pregnancy with a smile. I loved being pregnant. I was in awe of my changing body and the thought that a life was growing inside of me. I was blessed to have a textbook pregnancy; every test and measurement taken was perfect at every checkup. I was nauseated for the first trimester, but it wasn't bad. I vomited only once, because I took a pre-natal vitamin without food. I felt more beautiful being pregnant than I had ever felt in my life.

I didn't have any wild cravings, but I did want one orange every night after dinner. I'd sit back in the recliner and put the peelings on a paper plate set on my enlarged belly. As I ate the orange and the nutrients made their way to Ava, she started moving, causing the plate of peelings to teeter on top of me. It was blissful to watch and my favorite time of the day. I never felt alone when she was inside me.

Matt's level of protection skyrocketed during my pregnancy. While rollerblading he literally circled me with his arms out in case I fell. It was silly, because I wasn't far along, I was good on blades, and the trail was clear and flat. Another time he walked in the door and saw me on a step stool, maybe two feet high, and he practically had a heart attack as he rushed to usher me back down to the floor.

We had a coed baby shower, which I later referred to as Matt's Comedy Hour. He was ecstatic during the party and kept telling jokes and funny stories. It was the most fun I'd ever had at a baby shower and the only one where I'd seen men in attendance. We knew it was an unusual idea, but we never thought that welcoming a child into a home should exclude the father.

When Ava finally arrived, it was one of the happiest days of our lives. Matt presented our hours-old baby with a Tiffany's infinity necklace. He wrote in a card to her, "A Father's love is infinite and I will always be here for you. Welcome to our family. Love, Daddy."

Lucky girl. I didn't even know Tiffany's offered anything other than lamps until I was out of high school, and I certainly didn't get anything in that famous blue box until I met Matt. I was happy that the first man to buy her jewelry was one of Matt's caliber.

He didn't forget about me the day Ava was born. When I was seven months into my pregnancy, my fingers had swollen too much to wear my wedding ring, so I had to take it off. Matt took the opportunity to sneak the ring away and upgrade my one-stone solitaire by adding two more diamonds and then resetting it in platinum. He presented me with the three-stone diamond ring at the hospital. We were five months short of our ten-year anniversary, so the ring was for both Ava's birth and our milestone year. It was beautiful and he was excited to present it to me. I was groggy with pain medication, so when I opened the gift box, my reaction was quite minimal. Poor guy; he was totally deflated. We chuckled at that memory many times.

As Ava grew, Matt took her everywhere to show her off. He was proud of her and loved when people commented on how much she looked like him. To this day she still does. She remains the spitting image of him, and I love it. Matt even bought his own diaper bag. It was olive green and definitely masculine, but he never viewed his daughter's care as women's work. He never once referred to watching his own daughter as babysitting. Matt approached everything that way. He was either all in or he was out.

You might think that because of his gentle and compassionate nature he was a soft man. He was, with Ava and me, but otherwise he was as tough as they come. He was his father's son and a Marine. He had an impressive build, broad shoulders, and a barrel chest. God help anyone who was aggressive toward a friend of Matt's or me. He was fearless and protective and made it clear no one was allowed to talk down to someone in his company. He would adapt a stern tone of voice and walk with a purpose *toward* the aggressor. I never saw him physically fight anyone, because the few times he reared up to defend someone, the other guy always backed down.

26

April 2011

At times when I told someone that my husband was a pilot, I'd get the response, "Doesn't that scare you?" I always thought the question was an ignorant one. I knew the statistics; the estimated chance of dying in a plane crash is one in eleven million. You have a greater chance of being kicked to death by a donkey than dying in a plane crash. *How could he have died in a plane crash?* Obviously his chances were increased because of his job, but I still never thought it would happen.

I noticed a layer of dust blanketing the side tables in my bedroom. I decided it was time to give the house a thorough cleaning. As I did, a knot formed in my stomach, because I realized Matt was disappearing. *When will I vacuum the last strand of his hair or piece of his fingernail? When will I wipe away the last of his fingerprints? When will I polish away every last particle of his DNA? Is today the day? Will this day mark the removal of all bodily evidence of his life?* I dusted the photos but could not bring myself to look at his image. It hurt too much. I was tired of crying.

I didn't want the splitting headache or the dry, fiery eyes that followed.

I heard a ballad playing on the radio with the words, "I'd die for you." I was immediately submerged in anger as quickly as a rock thrown in a lake. I screamed, "F*** you!" at the radio. "Only a f***ing idiot would say that, because you clearly don't know the hell you'd leave her in. Humph, you'd die for her? Do her a f***ing favor and let her die, dumb ass."

I read that the root of all anger is fear. *If that's so, what am I afraid of? Being too strict with Ava and failing as a parent? Yes. Making the wrong decisions because I don't have Matt's input? Yes. Being alone the rest of my life? Yes. Will I always be bitter, wanting only what I once had? Yes.*

The sweet, perfect life I once cherished was over. Sorrow washed over me and seeped into every atom in my body. I was back in bed, my head covered by pillows. I gave in. I was defeated. The first flutter of acceptance that he was gone settled into my bones.

* * *

At the end of a New Hope session, one of the counselors pulled me aside while the kids ate a snack. "This is the first time Ava has shown any strong emotion when talking about her father. She really broke down tonight. I took her in another room and rocked her. She only pulled herself together a few minutes ago."

"What happened?"

"We were sharing all the enjoyable things we used to do with the person who passed away. She started talking about

Sea World and the zoo and burst into tears. As I rocked her, I asked her to tell me more about her dad. All she would say was that she missed him."

Driving home, I asked Ava, "How was your meeting tonight?"

"Fine."

"What did you talk about?"

"Just who died."

"What did you say?"

"I don't want to talk about it."

We prepared for bed, and I let her sleep with me. I wanted to cuddle with her and be there if she decided to open up, but she didn't.

* * *

Three days later I had dinner plans with some friends, so my friend Gina's daughter came over to babysit. I returned in a couple hours and the babysitter told me that everything went well but Ava got locked in the bathroom.

"Okay, so she couldn't unlock the door?"

"No. She was inside and said she couldn't unlock it, so I called my mom over."

I thought it was odd that she couldn't unlock the door. I figured she might have put lotion on her hands and the lock was too slippery, so I didn't think anything more of it.

The next morning Gina called me to talk about what happened. "They were in the toy room drawing on the whiteboard. Ava suddenly stopped, stood for a moment, and then walked into the bathroom and locked the door."

"That's odd," I said. "We don't lock our inside doors."

"When my daughter went to check on her, Ava said she couldn't come out because the door was locked. She said she couldn't unlock it either, so I went over and used a pin to open the door. She was sitting on the edge of the tub, and she looked really sad."

"Oh no! What did you do?" I asked.

"I brought her to the sofa and held her for about thirty minutes. She didn't want to talk, but then she popped up and went back to playing in the toy room as though nothing had happened. She was fine the rest of the night."

I didn't put the incidents together until our next counseling session at New Hope. When it was my turn to talk, I relayed the story. I learned that if children had a breakthrough in counseling, it could manifest in the child later, even up to weeks later. Something she did or thought of in the toy room reminded her of the session three days earlier, and she worked through it by escaping to the bathroom.

27

May 2011

It was the beginning of May, and my neighbors invited us to their daughter's first communion. We attended the church service and ceremony, returned home, and walked over to the party that followed at their house. All the families in the neighborhood were there, the families Matt and I used to hang out with as a couple. Everyone was there but Matt. I felt angry and sad.

I couldn't handle sitting with everyone at the table anymore, so I took a lawn chair and put it by the bouncy house under the guise of supervising the children. They didn't need supervision, and everyone knew it. I just wanted to be alone. I put my back to everyone. I convinced myself they'd all be happier anyway, because they wouldn't have to worry about saying the wrong thing in front of the widow. Knowing my mood, I was also afraid I would bite off someone's head for no reason. No one should have had to be around me.

Later that evening I was combing Ava's hair before bedtime and she asked if she could stay up late.

"No, Ava. Tomorrow's a school day, and you need to get to bed on time."

"No, Momma. You said after the party I could stay up late because it's like a holiday."

I stopped brushing her hair. Memories of conversations we'd had over the past few months zipped through my head. In all of them, Ava asked for special favors. When I'd answer "No," she told me I had said "Yes" earlier. She said with complete conviction that I had already agreed to whatever it was she was asking for. Because I was in such a fog and couldn't rely on my memory, I'd go with whatever she said I had promised, even if it seemed unusual. It hit me like a tidal wave that Ava had been using my grief to manipulate me.

I met her reflection in the mirror and said very evenly, "No, Ava. What I said was that it's too bad the party wasn't on a Saturday, because if it were, I'd let you stay up later than usual." Our gaze remained locked.

She could tell by my expression that I was on to her. Her face dropped. She knew the gig was up and that mom was back.

* * *

The day before Mother's Day, my friend Gina said she was running some errands and wanted to know if Ava could join her.

"Sure," I said, happy she'd be occupied for a while.

The next morning I woke up feeling forlorn and thinking of how great Mother's Day was when Matt was here. He would go overboard with gifts and flowers. I thought of the previous year when he bought matching summer dresses for Ava and me and then took us to brunch.

Ava bounded into my room and said, "Happy Mother's Day!"

I smiled and gathered her up in bed with me. "Why thank you, my dearie!"

She pulled something from behind her back, a present wrapped beautifully. *How odd.*

"Here, Mommy," she said as she handed it to me, barely containing her excitement.

I opened it to find a gorgeous necklace with a heart charm. An orange stone was set inside the heart. "Ava, where did you get this?"

"Me and Ms. Gina got it yesterday. I picked this one because orange is your favorite color," she said with a huge smile.

I fought back tears as I hugged her and thanked her. I told her I was the luckiest mom in the world because I had the most perfect daughter. We dressed for church in the previous year's dresses from Matt and followed with a fabulous brunch. *Thank you, Gina.*

28

June 2011

I braced myself to open and clean out Matt's dresser drawers. I threw away his socks, T-shirts, and underwear. I cleaned the best of his workout gear, shoes, and belts for donation. It was a start and all I could do. I couldn't sort through his clothes in the closet yet, the ones I pictured him wearing when I thought of him.

* * *

I was having technical issues with my cell phone, so I visited the store to get some direction. My heart pounded because I knew someone there might look through my phone and see that I'd brought back all the deleted voice mail and text messages from Matt.

The tech asked a few questions as he bounced around on my phone. "You seem to have a lot of voice mail messages saved from one number. If you delete them, it'll help with your memory and speed."

"Yeah, aah ... I know, but umm ... but I can't delete them."

"You can always pull them up another time," he said, still looking at the phone.

"But I can't take the chance I'd lose them. They're from my husband ... he died." My voice cracked, I was barely breathing, and felt faint. I grasped the counter to steady myself.

He looked up from my phone and paused with a look of concern. "It's understandable that you'd want to save these, but you should save them on a computer. There's a great website–www.decipher.com. If you go there you can download software that'll allow you to save all the voice mails and text messages onto your hard drive. I highly recommend it. It'll run you about thirty dollars."

I did exactly as he instructed. Even though I'm technically challenged, I downloaded the software and saved every text message and voice mail from Matt from the previous two years. I did have to call the help hotline a couple times, but the representatives were knowledgeable and patient. The text messages were saved in message bubbles, just as I would see them on my phone. I felt relieved and ecstatic.

* * *

I moved my wedding ring to my right hand. It broke my heart, but I felt the time was right. I acknowledged that I was not married anymore, and even putting that thought together brought tears to my eyes. I never wanted to be unmarried. The transfer to the wrong finger was uncomfortable in more than one way, but I refused to not wear the ring at all. It's beautiful and represented a beautiful marriage. The time elapsed for me to move my ring to my right hand equaled that of a full pregnancy, the same amount of time to create a healthy baby. That day did not mark the creation of something, however. It marked the destruction of our marriage.

29

July 2011

Like a Weeble toy, I was often knocked over by depression, but I kept popping back up. Sometimes I was down for days; other times it was only one day. I continued to fall to the deepest point of depression each time, but as I grew stronger, I bounced back more quickly.

I had a streaming tape of everything I was grateful for running through my mind at all times. I used this method to cope. I reminded myself that I was in the best possible place when the tragedy happened. I was thirty-nine with life experience and clarity I would not have had ten years before. I had Ava. She was in the age range considered the easiest age for a child to lose a parent. I had a supportive network of friends, family, and neighbors surrounding me. We were healthy financially. I worked for a compassionate company when Matt passed and was able to stop working six months later.

I thought of the countless people who had lived through worse and lost more than I did, people without friends, faith, or resources to pull them through, the people living in a world void of hope, a world so horrible they'd gladly exchange their tragedy for mine, even for a day. I thought of people who lived in war-torn countries under cruel governments, people without clean water and who didn't know where their next meal would come from, children who were sold into the sex trade at tender ages to be used over and over again. I thought of grade-schoolers tormented by bullies that chipped away at their spirit every day and people who didn't know what it was like to feel loved.

I reminded myself that I had enjoyed unconditional love from a great man. I knew what it felt like to be cherished. I knew true love. I had been completely vulnerable to someone without fear of rejection or ridicule for even a minute. To have that kind of love for just one year would have been a great gift, and I had it for eighteen years.

Counting my blessings eased most of my depression but not all of it. On the saddest days, I could not console myself with thoughts of gratitude. I chastised myself for being thankful the day before. I ridiculed myself for the pathetic ramble I'd been on, by trying to use gratitude to cope.

The devil himself stood on my shoulder and yelled in my ear, "What a crock of shit! What about Ava, huh? Was she blessed by losing her father when she was four years old? Was Nancy blessed to lose her only son? A child molester somewhere is alive and shooting a video right now, but Matt is dead. Where is the justice in that situation? What have you got to be thankful for? You don't deserve what you had to endure. You'll never find another like him. No one will ever love you the way he did."

Days with the devil in my ear were my greatest battle. I felt forsaken. It took everything I had not to give in to the warming call of anger and self-pity. Trust me, caving in would have been much easier.

Only faith pulled me through the worst days. By faith I mean I wholly trusted God's decisions regarding my path and purpose in this life. Believing in God and trusting in God are two separate concepts. To vow complete trust in God is on a different level from saying, "I believe in God." Belief does not make trust automatic. I came to realize that when I was angry with God and struggled to accept the hand I had been dealt, I never stopped believing in him, but I did not trust him.

* * *

Many of my neighbors had rented condos at New Smyrna Beach for the week of July Fourth. The beach is only an hour away, and Ava and I were invited to join them for a few afternoons, but we drove back home at night. I was happy to be there because I love those people and Ava was having a blast.

Everyone was in a great mood, the weather was perfect, great music played, and we had plenty of food and drinks. Matt's absence put a damper on my mood, and I couldn't help being a bit withdrawn. I knew my friends noticed, but they didn't push me to do anything but sit in the sun. When I wanted to be alone, I walked up to the pool and told everyone I was going to check on the kids. Everyone understood.

My friends Carrie and Reeli joined Ava and me the evening of July Fourth for the fireworks display close to my home. Carrie brought her two sons so the kids could play. I was appreciative that friends remembered us on every holiday and significant day that first year, even the Fourth of July. It was quite a drive for both Carrie and Reeli, and their return home was late.

* * *

Mid-July represented the annual pilgrimage of Matt's fraternity brothers to the north woods of Wisconsin. It was always a great bonding time for the guys, and Matt had looked forward to it every year. While growing up, he always wished he'd had a brother, and found that being a Fiji was as close as he could get to actually having one. He treasured the camaraderie, friendship, and encouragement the men shared.

I boxed the majority of Matt's cherished Tommy Bahama wear, consisting of silk shirts, T-shirts, and sweaters, to send to the cabin for his friends. I knew Matt would have wanted his friends to have them. I framed copies of a photo collage for each of the guys, and I topped off the package with a bottle of Johnny Walker Blue, in hopes they would raise a glass in Matt's honor.

The package represented the first of Matt's finer clothes that I gave away. I'd broken the seal, so I barreled on and continued to clean out his side of the closet. I kept my five favorite Tommy Bahama silk shirts to have repurposed into scarves for Ava and me. I boxed up the best of what was left

for family members and prepared the remainder for donation. The job was done. It was not as horrible as I thought
it would be, because I did it when I was ready.

After Matt's fraternity brothers returned from their
weekend together, a couple of the guys sent thoughtful
e-mails thanking me for the gifts. They let me know they did
indeed toast their brother, and they all felt his spirit had been
there with them. I treasure these e-mails and will share them
with Ava someday. *Thank you, Eddie, Dave, Jared, and Pete.*

* * *

I decided to plan a road trip for the very end of July
that would take Ava and me into the first week of August.
Matt's and my wedding anniversary was approaching on
August 3, and it would have been our fifteenth year. I
scheduled our route so that I'd be with my friend Renee in
Cincinnati on the notable day. I knew Renee before I met
Matt, so she heard all about our first dates and was eventu-
ally a bridesmaid in our wedding.

We called our road trip the SODA Tour, the Summer
Of Dawn and Ava. Ava loved road trips, because they were
the only time I'd let her watch movies and snack all day. The
plan was to visit six separate friends whose distance made it
hard for them to visit us. I knew they quietly worried about
us. I wanted them to know I appreciated their support and
let them see we are doing okay, not just hear me say it over
the phone.

Our second stop was at my friend Sarah's place in Ohio.
We arrived in the early evening after our longest driving

day of the whole trip. We were hungry and a bit frazzled. Sarah suggested we go to a casual pizza place down the street, eat, come back, and relax. In maybe thirty minutes, we were at a table with pizza and drinks in front of us. *Ah, this feels good.* Ava seemed distracted as she alternated between eating and coloring her kid's menu while Sarah and I caught up.

"How are you, Dawn?" Sarah asked.

We hadn't spoken face to face since the previous December. She's a great friend, so her question wasn't confrontational, but I couldn't hide the sting of sadness her question brought. I could have, if we were on the phone. In seconds, her sheer concern crumbled my protective wall.

My voice wavered as I responded, "I'm doing okay. I still have some bad days; in fact I'm a little surprised at how bad some are—still. Lots of anger ... I just really miss him."

Ava shook her head and said, "Now she'll start crying like a baby," without looking up from coloring. She put a twang to the word *crying* to emphasize her frustration with me.

For an awkward pause neither of us responded. Sarah seemed surprised by Ava's words, but I was not. I knew my daughter just wanted my bereavement over. She didn't want me sad anymore. I would have loved to be over it too, but I knew I had a long way to go.

* * *

Another stop was to see a good friend of Matt's from flight school. He is married to another friend of ours, and they have two young girls. He told me how he heard the news about the accident and how painful it was. He shared that he felt so bad for Ava that he could hardly look at her at the funeral, knowing what she had lost. His words mean a great deal to me, because they showed his deep care and admiration for Matt and also our daughter. *Thank you, Brian.*

I learned that when I spoke to people after some time had passed since the funeral, they wanted to tell me how they heard the tragic news and how it made them feel. They wanted to share how devastated they were. They needed to give their homage to the deceased, to help themselves heal. I let them. It was their gift to me, even though it was hard to hear. I did not deny them the opportunity, and I would encourage other grievers to do the same.

30

August 2011

Our anniversary date arrived on the third. Thoughts of our wedding and previous anniversaries ran through my head all day. The memories were not all sad, though, because many brought a smile to my face. I was glad to be at Renee's house, so when I needed to walk away for a moment, I could. She'd keep an eye on Ava.

My mind drifted back to the day Matt and I went to get our marriage license. I was very happy but a bit distracted by the work I needed to complete for the college summer course I was taking. Not Matt. He was bursting with exuberant joy and kept smiling and cracking jokes at the courthouse. The women in the office were getting a kick out of him and couldn't help being pulled in by his infectious happiness. When one asked him his name, he took a breath, puffed out his chest, cocked his head upward, and said, "Mufasa!"

We all chuckled and shook our heads.

"You two will be married forever," she said, "because you laugh so easily. I can always tell who's going to make it and who isn't."

We got our license shortly after the Disney movie *The Lion King* came out. Although it was animated with children as the target audience, Matt and I loved it. Mufasa was the main character, a lion cub that inaccurately blames himself for his father's death. He runs away from the pride but eventually returns in triumph to follow in his father's footsteps.

After leaving the courthouse that day, I asked Matt why he'd said "Mufasa." He took my hands and smiled. "That's how I feel today, Dawn. I feel like I'm king of the jungle. I can't believe I get to marry you."

* * *

On August 6, Ava and I returned from our road trip. We had a great time and ended up logging 2,076 miles over nine days. Ava enjoyed the children's museums in both Columbus and Cincinnati, Ohio. She had fun playing with my friend's children and pets. Everyone we visited was thoughtful and gentle with us, and I was glad we went.

I felt an overwhelming need to see some of the anniversary cards Matt and I exchanged through the years. I looked through the ones I'd saved, and a sharp pain stabbed my core, right under my rib cage, as though I were being impaled. The pain radiated throughout my torso, conjoined with extreme sadness. I cried in a whimper because anything more than a shallow breath exacerbated the pain. I felt lonely without my best friend.

I plodded to his nightstand and opened the top drawer, because I knew he'd kept many cards and notes from me there. It was the first time I'd opened the drawer since his death. I still retained a nagging fear that he didn't know how much I really loved him. I was elated to read that I'd written over and over again how much he meant to me and how I loved him like I'd loved no other. The fear that he didn't know I loved him was calmed and never returned.

I continued to look through the drawer and came upon a receipt for season tickets to Sea World Orlando. I could see by the date that he bought them for the three of us right before he left for his final, fatal trip. I chuckled with joy and shook my head at yet another example of Matt's spoiling his girls. I had only a couple weeks to go before they expired. We got dressed and covered ourselves in sunscreen, giddy about our spontaneous trip to the theme park.

* * *

The next morning I flipped through my accumulated stack of mail and found a card from my mother-in-law that arrived on our anniversary. The greeting expressed an acknowledgment of tough days and encouraged me not to live up to anyone's idea of what I should do or be. It urged me just to be myself and reminded me that I was strong and that she believed in me.

She also wrote her own message regarding how joyful our wedding day was. She told me Matt often spoke of how much he loved, respected, and admired my strength of character. She thanked me for coming into his life, because I made it rich and meaningful, and that was all any mother could ever want for her child. She said that when Ava came into our lives, Matt didn't know until then how much more love he could give, and that Ava was a product of us. She closed by telling me to remember the joy, even while feeling the pain.

I was overwhelmed and happy to read her kind words. I vowed always to remember our wedding day with joy, alongside the sadness. Only the most precious of mothers-in-law could have sent this card to her daughter-in-law on such a tumultuous occasion.

* * *

It was the first part of August and the one-year anniversary date of Matt's death was less than a month away. I was edgy; I couldn't focus; I couldn't sleep; and I was easily irritated. My adrenaline was racing, and I seemed to have a headache all day, every day. The eczema on my face was flaring again, raw and painful. *Why am I upset? I wanted the year mark to arrive, so what is going on? I've got three weeks to go. I cannot be this much of a mess for that much longer.*

* * *

Ava was entering kindergarten that year, so she and I went to the orientation and school tour. It was mostly mothers with their children, but a few dads were there too. I felt sad. Ava didn't seem to be feeling sad at all; she was excited to catch up with some friends from pre-K.

I scanned a list to see who her teacher would be, and Ava and I walked to her classroom. Upon entering, Ava was shown where to sort her school supplies and asked to decorate a nametag for her new desk. I too was given a task to fill out the information and emergency contact sheets. My heart fell when I saw I needed to fill in her father's name, occupation, and phone numbers. I finished all areas of the contact sheets except Matt's information. I took a deep breath and scribbled the word Deceased next to Father's Name. Now I needed to meet the teacher.

Mrs. Camp looked like the ideal teacher you would want for your kindergartener. She was a few years from retirement and radiated warmth and kindness. She reminded me of a younger Mrs. Claus, and I was happy she was Ava's homeroom teacher. Nevertheless, my heart pounded and I was chilled with dread, having to tell her about our family. She greeted me with a big smile as she reached her hand toward mine.

"Hi, Mrs. Camp, I'm Dawn Bell and my daughter Ava is over there in the pink dress."

Before she had time to respond, I thrust the contact sheets toward her, pointed to the word *Deceased,* and blurted out, "Her father ... my husband ... died last September. She's handling it pretty well, but please remember this when you talk about families." *Am I breathing?*

"I will. I'm so sorry," she said sincerely and moved to hug me. I stiffened but hugged her back for just an instant before pulling away. My eyes welled with tears, and I knew if I blinked they would roll down my face. I wanted to accept her unspoken invitation to talk with her and unload some sadness. Instead I remained cold and withdrawn, so I wouldn't fall apart.

My reaction was often the same when I came across sweet and gentle people, some I knew, but some were strangers. They sensed others' pain and exuded a deep and genuine concern. They wanted to make whatever hurt feel better. They were willing to take on another's pain so that it was not all shouldered by the one who was hurt. I wanted to curl up in a ball and cry for hours while I told Mrs. Campbell everything, but instead, I swallowed my emotions and called Ava over to meet her. I could not get out of the building fast enough.

* * *

It was the third week of August, and the edginess, irritation, insomnia, and day-long headaches I'd experienced for two weeks amplified. *What? I've got another ten days before September 3. I've been a mess for two weeks straight, and I'm at the end of my rope.* I was weak and frazzled. I racked my brain for an explanation and finally realized what was going on. My last full day with Matt was August 24. He left for his trip very early the next morning. *This date is what is upsetting me. My body and mind are dreading that date, preparing me for it. The twenty-fourth is going to be a horrible day for me.* I had been so focused on the one-year mark that I didn't even consider our final day together in August would be a more painful date.

Our subconscious takes care of us, prepares us for a strenuous day. I had no reason to believe that August 24 would prove to be one of my worst days to come, but my body warned me. Because of the heads-up, I was able to prepare somewhat for the day and handle it better than I would have, had I not been forewarned. Our bodies know things that we may not.

The two weeks before and the morning of August 24 were horrendous. During my first year of grieving, I'd be really upset on the days leading up to a holiday or significant day, but once it arrived, I slowly calmed and decompressed as the hours and days wore on.

* * *

On the last Saturday in August, I had plans to meet Reeli for dinner. It had been a tough month, and it would be good for me to get out with a close friend. On the drive to the restaurant, my car was overcome with the smell of Matt's cologne. I'd know this scent anywhere. I kept sniffing the air and moving my head around as if trying to detect a gas leak. I wanted to be sure it wasn't a figment of my imagination. It was not, and I sensed his presence. I was stunned, nervous, and a little afraid. My breathing became shallow and my senses sharpened. I wanted to speak, but I thought I should just listen. Nothing happened except that I was calmed.

I somehow arrived safely at the restaurant. I parked and sat and listened. I felt wrapped in a big, warm hug, and tears sprung to my eyes. I sat still. Nothing happened. I shook myself out of my trance and joined Reeli for a nice meal and easy conversation. When we first sat down I couldn't wait to tell her what just happened, but we started talking about something else and we jumped from topic to topic as girlfriends do. As dinner continued I began to doubt what happened in the car. *If I tell her about it, she might think I'm crazy. She'll worry about me. Maybe it didn't really happen.* I didn't tell her.

After dinner I went back to my car. I sat for a minute and sniffed the air. Nothing. *Oh no, I am crazy.* I started the engine and pulled on the seatbelt. It stuck. "Matt?" I asked aloud. I was instantly swarmed with his scent again, but this time I had no fear, just an extraordinary feeling of joy. Tears welled in my eyes, because I knew he was with me and I knew I was not crazy. I sat and absorbed everything I was sensing. I don't know how long I sat there, maybe twenty minutes.

I spoke aloud to him. I asked him questions and told him I needed his guidance. "Please help me. Please come into my dreams and talk to me." I didn't hear a response, and he did not appear in my dreams for another two years, but that night I felt peace and a sense that I needed to trust the decisions I was very capable of making.

* * *

At the end of the month I received a long letter from another of Matt's friends from flight school. He shared his deep concern for Ava, Matt's mother and sister, and me. He told how he heard the news and how it affected him. His words were thoughtful and moving.

He wrote of meeting Matt at flight school and later flying with him when they both worked for a commercial airline. He shared story after story about the good times and the many laughs they had together. None of the stories were news to me, because I'd heard Matt tell the same stories, but I was happy to have them in writing.

He wrote "Matt was a true professional in every sense of the word and treated his crew with respect. I witnessed his command and was truly impressed in his confidence …. He had it all; a great family that he loved, a nice home, and the best aviation job (that we all wanted). And he knew it. It was obvious that he was truly smelling the roses. He was never pretentious about his good fortune, and he wasn't shy, either, to say that he knew what was most important in life - his family."

The closing of his letter was priceless. He offered to talk to Ava about her father as the years went by. This offer meant a great deal to me, and I will definitely take him up on it some day. I've read this letter many times, and it always affects me deeply. *Thank you, Reid.*

31

Twelve to Eighteen Months Without Matt
September 2011 - March 2012

At last the year mark arrived. The horrible sadness I felt in August had retracted to the level that had become my daily norm. Unfortunately, the day was not the pivotal moment I was hoping for. I'd hoped something would click, and I'd feel sincere hope. I felt only a slight sense of relief from the anniversary. I busied my thoughts by lining up the hours of the day to the hours of the same day, a year before. I remembered what happened at each hour the previous year, as time ticked by.

I savored this year's morning hours as they lined up with those of a year earlier, the few hours before the first phone call from UPS, before I knew. I tried to appreciate fully the final hours Matt was still alive the previous year, exactly one year later. I did this not only to acknowledge his last hours, but also mine. Those hours were my last, too, the last hours of the idyllic life I was living, before my world shattered, before I realized I would not grow old with Matt. We would never celebrate our twenty-fifth or fiftieth wedding anniversaries. We would not move our daughter into her first dormitory room or attend her wedding together. I would never see the joy on his face when he held his first grandchild.

* * *

On the ten-year anniversary of the 9-11 terrorist attacks, many news programs replayed footage from that horrible day that scars our nation's history. Seeing a plane crash into the towers hit me so much harder than it had ten years earlier. I jerked my head away from the screen in horror as my adrenaline spiked and my heart slammed in my chest. First responders and others who were there recounted that day, where they were, what they saw, and what was going through their heads.

I felt an unprecedented level of sympathy for the victims and survivors of the senseless attack, but I also felt envious. I was puzzled and surprised at first, so I thought it through. They had the support of the world. They and their children were enveloped in immediate care. I imagined they had professional assistance in many steps of their journey, when they were in the stifling fog of shock. They likely didn't have to explain their story over and over and be questioned as to when and where and how it happened. Their children weren't the only ones that lost a parent.

I'm not saying their grief or pain or journey was any less than mine, nor am I minimizing the support I had.

I'm simply making an honest observation of an individual versus societal tragedy.

* * *

I hated being single. The loneliness was crushing. I was tired of being alone and doing everything myself. I swore I would agree to an arranged marriage, sight unseen. My stomach roiled at the thought of dating again, having to start over. I would be willing to marry a stranger, as long as he promised to carry in the groceries and unclog some drains. I didn't have to love him, and he didn't have to love me.

But I didn't want just anybody. I wanted Matt. Only Matt. Him coming into my life was such a gift, and I met him when I was twenty-two years old. I loved being married to him. I loved the comfort and peace that marriage provided. I loved saying "my husband." I felt blessed to have a happy marriage and not be out on the market looking for Mr. Right. I had him, and I knew it.

Loneliness is dangerous and can lead to poor decisions and bad relationships, so I ignored men. If they made eye contact and smiled, I looked away. If they tried to talk to me, I was friendly, but my answers were short and I walked away as soon as possible. I knew that becoming involved with someone new would only delay my grieving process, and I was not ready, anyway. As they say, "Fall in love when you're ready, not when you're lonely."

I wanted to talk about Matt in almost every conversation I had. I wanted to include him in everything I talked about, because he was the best part of any story. If asked about a place I'd traveled to or a movie I'd seen, it seemed wrong not to mention Matt, if he had been there. I wanted to share a great experience of ours from that trip or what he thought of that movie. I wanted to answer as I would have answered a year before, not revise my response and leave him out, as if he hadn't been there. It was a Catch-22. If I omitted him so the conversation wasn't awkward, I felt I was erasing him. If I included him in the conversation, I caught the flash of sadness in the eyes of people I was talking with.

It had been about six months since I'd left my job in March. I was in such a fog at the time that it took me weeks to realize I was not going to work the next day. I spent a great summer with Ava, and she had entered kindergarten two months prior. I was not used to being a stay-at-home mother. I had already cleaned and organized every inch of my house, and I needed something to fill my free time while she was at school.

When Matt was alive, we had planned to have one more child and then eventually adopt a third. I wanted to continue our course and was pleasantly surprised to learn I was still able to adopt as a single parent. I thought I would be an undesirable candidate since I was single, but apparently I was not. I began the weekly classes to become certified to adopt. I reasoned I had a lot of love and time to give to a child, and it would be nice for Ava to have a sister.

I also started volunteering at a local food store. It was a huge international operation that accepted donated goods and shipped them to third-world countries or sold them locally at a great discount to low-income families. My job was to sort the huge bins of bagged candy that local super-markets donated. I priced them and kept the shelves stocked. It was easy, mindless work and exactly what I needed.

The average Joe worked there, and sponsored programs helped people get back on their feet. One program gave jobs to people who had just gotten out of jail. It was an interesting culture, because everyone was friendly, but they minded their own business. I could tell their lives had not been easy, because they were hesitant to trust anyone. They didn't offer much information or ask many questions. I felt accepted with no pressure to tell my story. It was liberating.

I learned a valuable lesson there that I never expected. I'd been coping by reminding myself of the countless people in the world who had it worse than me, but they were nameless, faceless people. Where I volunteered, the people with difficult lives became tangible. It helped me to be in the company of people other than those who lived easy lives. The temptation to compare my grieving life to another's happy life was powerful and tended to fuel bitterness in me. Among my friends, I was the only one who had suffered such an extreme loss. Some days it affected my appreciation for them, because I was jealous. Sometimes I ignored their phone calls and texts or I canceled dinner plans for fear I'd be mean. It was a horrible feeling to bear envy toward the people I loved most in the world.

At the food store I stopped making poor-me compari-sons because we were all in pain. I heard whispers of why this one had been in jail or how that one lost her husband or that another person's only child hadn't spoken to her in forty years. We were all working through some kind of hardship, be it a physical or mental impairment, poverty, felony record, or loss. We didn't want to talk about it, and we were all making an effort to get our lives back on track. As I healed, I began to talk about my loss with a couple of my new friends there. Being able to talk was imperative to my healing and an unexpected gift.

* * *

I continued to journal my thoughts, because doing so brought me peace. Some of my behavior and actions were so cruel or shocking that I could only write about them, because I was embarrassed to speak them aloud. When I looked back over what I had written a year before, I could see what a mess I had been, and it scared me to know I'd fallen to such a depth. I was awestruck at reading the words of a woman who seemed like a stranger, but was actually me. I knew I was not out of the woods yet, but I was not as bad as I had been.

* * *

Ava was spending a Saturday night at a good friend's house, and I was happy to have a night to myself with sushi and a movie. A side story in the movie was about a writer attending a conference, and it stirred my curiosity. *Does Florida have a writer's conference? It must. It's probably in Miami.* Since my dream had always been to write, and I now had the time to concentrate on it, I grabbed my laptop and Googled Writer's Convention Florida. FWA popped up, the Florida Writer's Association. I clicked on it and learned the annual meeting was being held only a few miles from my house and was less than two weeks away. *It couldn't be any more convenient.* I applied for a three-year membership and registered for the conference.

A couple weeks later I arrived at the conference and picked up my registration packet. I was excited because it was a huge step toward a lifelong dream of being a writer. I didn't know anyone there, but I'd never been afraid of entering a room full of strangers. My only concern was how to skirt the usual questions, "What do you write?" "Are you married?" I decided I would answer that I wrote short stories, which was true. I didn't need to mention I might write a memoir someday, and I would say I was no longer married. I'd then close my mouth, lift my chin, and look the person in the eye so I was not asked a follow-up question. *You gotta love the power of body language.*

The conference was great and I attended many informative workshops. I found illustrators, editors, printers, and other vendors available to speak to, as well as literary agents representing all genres. Writers could pay for a ten-minute session to pitch their work to an agent. I was not at that point yet, but I considered I might be, next year.

* * *

Ava was enjoying kindergarten and had made many new friends. Reading with your child was being emphasized in the curriculum, and she was sent home with a new

Sunshine Reader book every week. One night I read to her while she was eating dinner. It was a cute little book about a boy standing in front of an elevator, and every time the doors opened, a different animal was standing inside. Each time the boy asked the animal a question, and the reader was prompted also to ask the animal a question.

We were giggling often, because Ava was coming up with some creative questions for the animals. We read to the end of the book and saw that when the elevator door opened up the last time, the boy's father was standing there.

I felt as though a sledgehammer had swung into my rib cage. *You've got to be f***ing kidding me.* I stopped breathing, I was paralyzed, and I didn't know what to do. I saw Ava's eyes had widened and her mouth had fallen open. Her fork was frozen midair as she stared at the page.

As if someone took us off Pause, I came out of my trance. I slowly read the boy's words, "Hi, Dad!" I turned to the last page and continued reading, "What would you say to your dad?"

Still staring at the book, she said, "It's nice to see you."

* * *

Ava wanted to try some after-school sports, and I attended practices with her. Between her activities and my volunteering a bit in her classroom, I'd met quite a few new people. I knew they wondered about my marital status, because they saw Ava, but I was not wearing a diamond on my left hand. Out of courtesy, most did not pry, so I came right out and told them, for two reasons. (1) So I could get it over with, and (2) Because I could not stomach the thought of someone thinking I was divorced. Even if I was meeting people for the first time and they had never met Matt, I wouldn't allow them to think I had ever divorced such an amazing man. I refused not to acknowledge our marriage. I had hidden the truth at the writer's conference, and I regretted it.

I had met many people in the past few months and was flattered that many wanted to meet up with me outside of school activities, church, our book club, or whatever brought us together. Never in my life had I had so much time to widen my circle of friends. I made a pact with myself to cast my friendship net widely and accept as many invitations as possible. I still was not sure what else I should be doing or how to identity myself without Matt, so I just showed up. Whether it was a lunch invitation, a volunteer opportunity, or getting our kids together, I showed up.

* * *

My friend Kristy brought me a book she thought might be helpful, Max Lucado's *Traveling Light*. I had never heard of him and was a bit sheepish to learn he was a big deal in Christian writing and ministry. The book looked solely at the promise of Psalm 23 and expounded on each verse. I hung on every word I read, especially verse four, "Yea, though I walk through the valley of the shadow of death, I will fear no evil; for You are with me; Your rod and Your staff, they comfort me."

Max Lucado shared his impressive ability to make horrible tragedy understandable, or at least bearable. He explained it from a point of view I had never considered. The book was a pivotal tool in my healing. I thought of all the times I had fallen on my knees, defeated by grief. If I pictured Matt, also on his knees, but in awe of God, my loss became endurable, because I knew he was immersed in a love that I could not even fathom. *Thank you, Kristy.*

I believe humans have the resilience to live through anything; we just need to find a way of looking at it in a way that makes sense to us. We don't even need to understand it completely, just be able to wrap our heads around it halfway. We can chalk the other half up to being beyond our comprehension. It helps to humble ourselves and understand that we are simple animals with limited capacity to make sense of all events in our lives.

Imagine if you had a beloved family pet that contracted an infection in its leg and the only way to save the animal was to amputate that leg. You would feel horrible about it, and you would wish you could explain to the animal what was happening and why, but it's incapable of understanding. Maybe that's how we are to God. He does everything in our best interest, even if it's painful or disfiguring, but he can't explain it to us, because we are unable to comprehend. We are left with the only viable option of trusting him and believing that some day we will understand. We either accept that, or we don't. There's no middle ground.

* * *

During our second Christmas season without Matt, I decorated the whole house and baked cookies. On Christmas Eve my brother David and his family joined us for a big meal and gift exchange. We had a great time, and I was happy for the distraction by being hostess most of the day. On Christmas morning Ava and I awoke and opened our presents. Shortly after, I was overcome by grief and returned to bed while Ava played alone. I was consumed with guilt, anger, and sadness. I could not get up. I heard Ava playing with toys and talking to her new stuffed animals. She dashed between the living room and my bedroom to share something she was doing with a new toy. I was able to mask my true emotions and faked a big smile for the few seconds to say, "Wow! That's awesome, Ava." It seemed to be enough for her. *Is it?* I buoyed back up after a few hours to make a great brunch and to play with her. Happiness crawled back at a sloth's pace as the day continued.

I badly wanted answers to my questions about Matt's death, but I knew they would come when they were supposed to, in this life or the next. I reflected on all my blessings and Max Lucado's words. I bowed to my grief and allowed it to run its course. I still carried around shackles of disappointment, rage, and sorrow. Some days it was barely manageable. Other days it stayed below the surface and just simmered, waiting to erupt.

For example, I was at the grocery store and annoyed with the length of the checkout line. The level of irritation and anger I felt was disproportionate to the circumstances, but I could barely contain it. I imagined the look on my face could turn a person to stone. I heard the bagger chatting with the person at the head of the line, but I couldn't see the two of them. His speech was odd, as if he were talking to a child or trying to be amusing, which infuriated me even further. How dare he hold a conversation when I needed him to work faster? *What is he, a retard?* I finally reached the front of the line and was ready to glare at the bagger. I felt justified in treating him with anger, because he should have been working faster. I looked at him and could see he had a physical handicap, and when he said "Hello" to me, he also had a speech impediment. My body shriveled in shame. I had to look away, because I couldn't even face him.

Typing this story three years later brought tears to my eyes at my vile behavior. I could still see his sweet face as he smiled and said, "Hello." Please know that *retard* is not a word I ever used or felt was acceptable to use. It was deplorable and wrong. I included this story only to demonstrate how grief unchecked caused me to become a person I did not even recognize and was certainly not proud of. The incident happened about a year and four months after Matt's death and substantiated the lasting effects of grief. It lingered for years, which is not to say grievers are unaccountable for his or her actions, but if you witness someone being vicious, he or she is probably dealing with a great deal of pain from somewhere.

* * *

I finished the twelve weekly adoption classes, did all the homework, had my fingerprints taken, and had my background checked. I needed only a few home visits, and I was ready to adopt a child. I began looking at websites for a child to add to our family and realized my prospects were limited. I wanted one child, but most available children were part of sibling groups. Some single children were available to adopt on the condition that the parent(s) were found unsuitable or gave up their rights. I would have to foster the child first and keep my fingers crossed, a chance I was afraid to take. I could not imagine bringing a child into my home only to have the child ripped away. Ava and I had lost enough.

One night I told Ava that getting her a sister wouldn't be as easy as I thought. She put her head down and said, "Mommy, I don't want a sister. I like just us."

How can I possibly argue with her? Ava's honesty, coupled with my recent behavior at the grocery store, told me it might not be the right time to pursue adoption. I was still dealing with too much anger, anger I was under the impression would last only a year. *That's the magical healing time frame, right?* Wrong. My moods and agitation would be unfair to a child who likely had not had an easy journey. I decided to stop the adoption process, but I would continue to donate my time and money to causes that supported abused and neglected children.

My certificate to adopt would be good for five years, and maybe I would change my mind in time, but Ava would have to be completely on board. I wanted to continue the course Matt and I were on, and I thought I should add a child to our family, but maybe I was trying to fill a void. I accepted that life evolves, and it's okay to change direction.

I did not regret having taken the classes. I learned a great deal about adult behavior based on childhood experiences, my own included. At forty years old, I finally understood why I did some things that were out of character in my twenties, things I was not proud of. I am accountable for my actions, but for the first time in my life, I forgave myself for questionable behavior in my past. Self-forgiveness brought me an unprecedented level of inner peace. My tolerance for others was growing too. Before taking the class I thought I was compassionate toward others. I was, but only toward those I deemed deserving. Now I try every day to be purposely compassionate toward those who honestly get under my skin. I am not always successful, but the days I succeed usually outnumber the days I fail.

* * *

On New Year's Eve, Ava and I walked the forty feet to our neighbor's house for a party. Ava was convinced she could stay awake to see the ball drop for the first time. All the kids had a great time playing, and I enjoyed talking with some interesting people. At around eleven o'clock, I realized Ava was not with the other kids. I found her fast asleep on the sofa. I knew she'd be disappointed she missed the countdown, so I tried to shake her awake and see if she would get her second wind. Not a chance. I was happy to go home early, because I couldn't ring in 2012 with a kiss from Matt anyway.

I thanked my friends for the invitation and told them I was going to get Ava in bed. One of the men offered to carry her for me, but I said I'd be fine. I realized halfway home that my child was heavier than I realized. *When did this happen?* I barely reached our back door before I had to rest on a chair. I finally slid her into bed and considered some resolutions. I needed to be able to carry Ava, and I owed it to her to take better care of myself physically. I had to do everything in my power to prevent disease and illness. If I died, I resolved not to let it be a result of something I could have prevented. If something happened to me, she would be an orphan.

I had always wanted to try Pilates, so I ordered some videos. They arrived early in the year, and I combined the workouts with treadmill runs. I had no idea Pilates was so hard, but after the initial two weeks of agony, I began to feel stronger and healthier. The exercise also increased my appetite and I had more interest in food than I had in a long time.

I still had many sad days marked by my refusal to accept kindness or support from my friends. Some days I isolated myself. Maybe I didn't have the strength to be civil or maybe I was punishing myself; I didn't know. On those days, even exercise couldn't lift my mood. My body fought it and every movement hurt.

One day I was reading on the sofa and dozed off. I was pulled from my slumber by the sound of someone typing on the keyboard in the office. I drew a quick breath and realized I thought it was Matt. It turned out to be Ava playing, pretending she was typing. I was shocked and profoundly disappointed to realize there was still a fraction of me that thought he could be alive. *Have I made no progress?*

Matt and I knew each other's passwords on all accounts, so I checked his Facebook page occasionally. I reread our text messages. I listened to his voice mails a couple times. If a funny or silly thing happened, I ached to share it with him. As time passed, my thoughts changed from *This is my husband* to *This was my husband.* The life we had together was over, but I didn't want Matt to be a memory. I fought it. I wanted him there.

Some nights I lay in bed and looked up at the steady green light on the smoke alarm. Beside it a red light flashed every twenty-five seconds. I imagined I was standing outside, looking up into the night sky at Matt's airplane. I pretended the smoke alarm lights were his wing tip lights; red on right, green on left. I fantasized that he was flying home to me. Some nights I let Ava sleep with me. I lay awake and heard her soft breathing, deep asleep beside me. I pretended it was Matt. It was futile, but I didn't care.

Some people say they have seen their loved ones in dreams and held a conversation with them or were given a message. I wished and prayed Matt would speak to me in a dream, but he never did. Many times I ran in circles trying to make a decision or drove myself crazy wondering if I was doing the right thing. I missed consulting him. I wanted to talk to him about things I would speak only to my husband about. It was a constant reminder of how alone I was.

* * *

At the end of March, Ava turned six years old. I brought a Hello Kitty cookie cake to her school at lunchtime and enjoyed eating with her. We had celebrated by going to Weekie Wachee Springs State Park with Ava's best friend, Mia. The park is on the gulf coast of Florida and was one of the nation's most popular tourist stops in the 1950s. It has always been known for its live mermaid shows. Ava and Mia were really into mermaids because *The Little Mermaid* had just been released, so the girls sat in awe during the show. Afterward, they had an opportunity to have their photo taken with a "real live" mermaid. They could hardly contain themselves.

We grabbed lunch at one of the restaurants and enjoyed watching the family of peacocks that resided on the property. The girls then played in the splash area while I sat in the sun with my ear buds and iPod. It was a wonderful day for all of us.

32

Nineteen Months to Two Years Without Matt
April – August 2012

I was getting dressed to attend a fundraiser that benefitted New Hope for Kids, the counseling center we had been going to. I was seized with panic at the thought that some of the doctors I used to call on as a sales representative might be there too. It wasn't that I didn't want to see them; they're great people. It was just hard to see people for the first time since the accident, especially in a public forum. I wondered what they might think if they saw me enjoying myself.

I considered the doctors I knew to be friends, and it was foolish to think they would judge me. This fear of judgment was my own issue. I felt guilty to be wearing a pretty dress, to enjoy talking with men at a party, or to have a great night out. I feared it appeared I didn't miss Matt or that I was disrespecting him by conversing with men who weren't him.

I ended up having a fabulous time at the fundraiser and saw no one I knew. What was funny was that when I returned home, I wished some of those doctors I knew had been there.

Many days I felt lightness more than grief. I reasoned I must have been healing, because I was able to laugh and smile more and more. My thoughts were validated when I spoke to five close friends individually over the course of a week or so. Each one shared something that had upset them recently. I was tickled. They must have thought I was better, if they were telling me they'd had a bad day. No friend wanted to share her bad day with me before, because it was trivial in comparison to my husband's death.

Ava and I were invited to the fiftieth wedding anniversary party for our cousins who live locally. While I was happy for them and happy to be there, I couldn't help pondering that I'd never be married for fifty years. Even if I remarried, I'd probably never reach twenty-five years of marriage either.

* * *

It appeared I was giving off some kind of vibe, because I was approached by a number of men over a few weeks' time. *Am I being punked?* I hadn't gotten this much attention since I was in the military, where the ratio of men to women was ten to one. I was flattered, but it was not what I wanted at the time. I told them all thank you, but I'm happily married. Oh, how I wished it were true. None of them asked why my diamond was on my right hand.

Ava told me she was ready for a new daddy. I couldn't imagine remarrying anytime soon. Besides, she might feel differently if a man in the house took some of my attention away from her. She was probably just tired of being different. *So am I.*

I continued to have sad days during which I avoided photos of Matt. Looking at his smiling face would bring me too much pain. On other days, I couldn't pull my eyes away from his picture.

The day before Mother's Day, we joined our friends Kristy and Marc and their kids at their community pool. I was grumpy, but I showed up because I wanted Ava to have fun. I could not focus enough to hold a conversation and was mortified to be tearing up behind my sunglasses. I kept my feelings inside, because otherwise I'd ruin everyone's good time. I felt my adrenaline kick in and could smell the horrible, concentrated sweat on me. I dove into the pool and wished I'd never come back up.

In the evening my mood took an upward turn as I made dinner and listened to music. It always helped to chop veggies and create something yummy in a warm kitchen. I loved almost all music, and I liked to listen closely to the lyrics to learn the story behind the words. Ava sat at the kitchen island and listened to me singing softly.

"Why is he singing about Georgia?" she asked.

"It was his home state and the only place he had his sense of vision. He went blind when he was young and was sent away to a school here in Florida. I suppose some of his best memories were from his childhood before he went blind."

"Why did he go blind?"

"I'm not sure. I saw a movie about him, and I think it was a virus, but he had an amazing life, Ava. His name was Ray Charles, and he could play the piano even though he couldn't see. He wrote a lot of songs, became famous, and traveled all over the world. He was also black, and when he was younger, black people weren't treated very well. One time he came back to Georgia to perform a concert. He was shocked to learn that only white people were allowed to come to his concert. He was so upset he canceled at the last minute and left. The people in charge were angry and barred him from returning to his home state. They wouldn't let him ever come back to Georgia."

"Why did they do that?"

"Because their hearts were full of hate for people that had dark skin. Even big people make bad mistakes, Ava. Anyway, Ray Charles sang this song about how much he loved Georgia, and even if he couldn't be there, he always thought about it. That's why he sounds sad; something he loved was taken away from him. Do you think he sounds sad?"

"Yeah. Did he lose his dad?" she asked.

I was taken aback because I actually hadn't considered Matt's coming into the conversation. I rewound to what I'd just said and sighed with disappointment at myself for not staying focused.

I took a quick breath. "I don't know. I'm sure he did at some point; but he did lose his brother. He drowned when he was a little boy."

"What? Why?"

"It was an accident. I think he was only about seven years old … but … your dad got to live to be thirty-eight. He had a really happy life for many years, Ava."

She concentrated on her little hands. "I know, Momma."

An Avril Lavigne song was on next, and Ava asked, "Why does she say he looks like a fool?"

I chuckled. How was I going to explain to a six-year-old that a teenage boy wanted to seem cool and not show vulnerability to someone who could break his heart?

"Well, he likes this girl but he doesn't want her to know, so he's acting like she's no big deal, even though he wants to talk to her."

"Why doesn't he just talk to her?"

"It's hard to explain, honey. I think he's afraid she won't like him back, and that would make him sad, so he's trying to get her attention so she will come talk to him."

"Oh," she said with a puzzled look on her face.

"When a Man Loves a Woman" by Percy Sledge played. "Ava, listen to these words," I said as I sang them.

"Why would he sleep in the rain?"

"Well, when a man finds the one woman who is perfect for him, he will do anything for her, just like in this song. If his friend says something bad about the girl, he won't be a friend to that person anymore. He will put the girl before everyone else, because he doesn't want to lose her. You know what? That's how much your daddy loved me. He would have done anything for me, Ava, and I loved him back just as much. That's why he asked me to marry him;

that's why he chose me. Some day you'll meet a boy who will love you sooo much, he'll ask you to marry him."

"Ewww! I'm not getting married."

"Oh, Ava, you don't have to, but some day you might want to. But that's many, many years from now."

We continued to listen to music and talked about many things. That night I lay in bed thankful for the unexpected guidance. I'd been concerned for Ava that she wasn't seeing how her dad treated me; she wasn't learning how she should be treated when she dated and eventually married. Our talk showed me she didn't need to witness it. I could teach her through music and my memories of Matt.

The next day I was heartbroken at seeing all the happy couples in church for Mother's Day. The yo-yo of emotions that weekend was killing me. It was sweet how the husbands and children were treating their wives and mothers, but I was filled with despair. I tried hard to end my pity party, but it was a challenge. My friend Marc brought me a beautiful arrangement of Mother's Day flowers later in the day when he picked up his daughter from a play date with Ava. *Thank you, Marc.*

* * *

Ava and I were at New Hope waiting for our session to begin. I had arranged ahead of time to have this session be our last. Seats were limited, so the preference was that you occupy a membership for two years and then pass your seat on to another. You could choose to leave earlier or stay longer as needed, and the door was always open to return. We had been attending for eighteen months, and I felt that Ava and I were in a good place emotionally. By coincidence, my phone beeped, and I saw an e-mail from Ava's kindergarten teacher. I fought tears as I read her kind message. When the session began, I asked if I could read it out loud.

Dawn,

I just wanted to tell you how amazing I think your daughter is. Yesterday I told her that we would write about our dads today. I asked her if she wanted to participate. I gave her some other options, but she chose to write about her dad. She joyfully shared a memory about him to the class. I know it must be difficult for you, but know how wonderfully she is processing the information with the world. I've learned a lot about her dad through her writing. She loved him a lot. She is an amazing little girl, and you are blessed to have her as a daughter.

Blessings to you both.

It was very hard to keep myself together as I shared the e-mail with the group at New Hope. Everyone responded with happiness for us. I was thankful for Ava's strength.

The counselor asked for my thoughts on why Ava was progressing so well. I responded that bringing her to this counseling center had been a great help. "Enough cannot be said about the importance to the child of not being the only one who no longer has her mother or father. We are blessed to have wonderful friends, neighbors, and teachers surrounding us. I also followed advice to keep the discussion door open. I encouraged her to talk and cry whenever she wanted, because Lord knows I do!

"Perhaps it's also the dynamics of our family. It's just the two of us, so I'm able to give her all my attention. She's had some tough times too, but she's coping well, and I'm happy to get this message."

Our counselor responded, "That is great, Dawn. I don't want to take any joy away from this moment, but let me take this opportunity to remind you all, even though your child is doing well for a time, it can always change. Many times young children's reactions to a death will not fully manifest until they're in their teens or even college. It happens during stressful times or when another loved one or an animal dies."

She's right.

A few days later, Ava came home from school with her Father's Day gift. It was a cute card thanking him for some of the great things they had done together. She wrote that she had fun and wished he could come back. We put it in a shoebox designated for Matt. She had previously decorated it with stickers, pictures, and bells. We put little gifts and photos in the box and kept it in a very safe place. Ava liked to take it down and look through it sometimes.

On June 16, 2012, the day before Father's Day. I was so sad that I could not focus. I could not talk. I felt intense anger. My heart actually ached as though in a vice. I could not breathe deeply enough to get sufficient oxygen. I felt like I was suffering an anxiety attack. I had to sit, because I thought I would faint if I stood.

On Father's Day I took Ava to Sunday school at our church. The children were presented with a Father's Day project. They were given a prewritten note to give to their fathers, but some words were missing. The children were told to fill in the blanks by gluing in bite-sized candy bars, also provided. When I picked her up she couldn't wait to show me her work. She read a sentence, "I would travel to (Mars) and the (Milky Way) for you," as we walked into the sanctuary. We sat, and Ava asked if she could eat the candy bars. I smiled at my little chocoholic. "You can have a couple now, but save the rest for later."

A woman sitting next to us teased Ava that she was eating the candy before her daddy could get it. We both smiled at her but didn't respond. Later that day I was straightening the house and returned Ava's shoes to her bedroom. I noticed her calendar was open on her bed and she'd written on that day's date, "Ava and Dawn cannot see Matt." She had drawn a sad face with tears. I felt sorry for my little girl. I could take anything you threw at me, but it killed me that my sweet, innocent child had to deal with such an extreme loss.

* * *

During the second half of June, I decided to get a tattoo. If you knew me, you knew this act was completely out of character. I never thought I would get a tattoo. I did not mind a few discreet tattoos on other people, but I'd never been a fan of them. Matt had four: a USMC tattoo on his upper right arm, the Eye of Horus on his upper left arm, and a fraternity tattoo on the inside of each of his ankles.

A few months after his death, I was looking through family photos and came across one of Matt in the pool. I could see his Eye of Horus tattoo clearly. For some reason, I became overwhelmed with a desire for the same tattoo. I had to have it. I remembered the day Matt had come home with it. He explained that it was the Egyptian god of war. Only a few months after his death, though, I knew I was in no condition to make such a permanent decision, so I decided that if I still wanted it in a year, I'd get it.

So there I was in a tattoo parlor, my body so clean of ink I looked like I'd walked in to ask directions to the library. I brought in an image of the tattoo. None of the artists jumped to do the work, because it was simple and boring compared to the multicolored, intricate examples on the wall each artist displayed. One artist finally offered to do the design for me. I had it downsized to a square inch and asked for it to be placed on the inside of my left arm, just below the elbow. I wanted it there because I was doing it just for me. I wanted to see it every day. I chose eggplant for the color, because Matt's favorite color was purple.

The job took only fifteen minutes and the pain was minimal. As soon as he finished, I looked in the mirror and was overjoyed. I touched it lightly as I would touch fragile crystal. An odd sensation came over me, as if I found something that had been lost, like I'd lost a necklace with great sentimental value that had just been returned to me. I felt a part of Matt had returned to me. *What took me so long?*

When I returned home I researched and learned that The Eye of Horus was one of the most common tattoos inked. Some believe it's a symbol of protection and power; some say it represents the god of war; and others say it represents the goddess of the sky. That last one made me chuckle at the thought of seeing Matt's face once he learned it represented a goddess. I learned the confusion stemmed from the Egyptians praying to the sky before an impending war for protection from the enemy's arrows and for success for their own arrows when shot. The symbol also represents the six senses—six, because the Egyptians recognized thought as a sense.

* * *

I continued to be spoiled by the great support of family and friends. My close friends and neighbors still looked out for us and included us in many activities and events. I still received text messages, e-mails, and phone calls from those who lived far away or those who weren't close friends but who did care about us. Yes, the expressions had waned over twenty months, but they still came in. It was also thoughtful that many of my friends had shared my story with their friends and family, and my friends told me that these people I had never met prayed for us and asked for updates on how we were doing. *The world is filled with amazing people. Thank you for your prayers.*

I was thankful to live in a time where there were many options for communication. Texting and e-mails allowed a person to check in without fear of imposing upon me. It was not especially personal, but that was okay. If it was the only way a person was comfortable reaching out, I would happily take it every time.

* * *

I still had difficulty enjoying holidays, even minor ones such as July 4. That year, the town I lived in was hosting a Celebration Party. The streets were shut down and filled with food trucks, beer stands, and live music. Face painting and animal balloons were available for the kids. I looked around and all I could see were kids and happy couples. I felt they were parading in front of me and throwing their joy in my face. I would rather have seen couples bickering and disrespecting each other. I wanted to believe no couple was truly happy.

I was irate and working myself into a frenzy. I was a ball of negative energy trying to infect everyone around me with the same negativity. When I bumped into someone in the crowd, I didn't excuse myself. When I stood in line for a drink, I didn't mask my disdain for having to wait. When I saw a man spit tobacco on the street, I looked at him in disgust. I wanted to yell at a mother to control her child, because I thought the toddler was too unruly. I wanted to tell her she didn't deserve to have children. I was reprehensible, but I couldn't stop.

I wanted to be mean and cause pain in everyone I encountered. On some level I thought if I did, I would force them to take some of my pain away from me, and then my pain would be lessened. The truth is that pain does not lessen that way. Pain multiplies when it's thrown at another, because a stranger's reaction is usually anger, and anger lives in the same house as pain.

I should have known better. I recognized the warning signals my body sent before I got there, but I chose to ignore them. My jaw was tense, I was stressed and impatient all day, and I had a pounding headache. In conversation my words and facial expressions were exaggerated. I should have stayed home and stopped the mudslide of emotions before they started, but I didn't. Why? Because it had been almost two years since Matt's death, and my ego refused to admit I was still grieving. *I should be over this.* I pushed myself to join in an activity when I should have stayed home. If I had, I could have dealt with my anger calmly, or at least in isolation, instead of attacking others.

In mid July, Ava and I vacationed at New Smyrna Beach for a week. A couple friends joined us for an afternoon here and there, but it was mostly just the two of us. One night Ava was in the bedroom playing with her stuffed animals. I was in the living room caught in a downward spiral of depression. I'm not sure what triggered the episode, but it was one of my worst, and it seized me without warning. I was filled with so much anxiety I couldn't sit still. Just like eighteen months earlier, I could not hold a thought in my head. It's hard to put into words, but I felt unsafe. Only a war zone could make me so tense, edgy, and frazzled. I felt as though I had to remain on high alert or I would be physically harmed.

Adrenaline torpedoed through me and caused all my muscles to twitch. Again my senses were heightened and everything was loud. When I looked out the sliding glass door, I swore I could hear a flower grazing the side of the building in the breeze, a breeze that sounded like a blast of wind. I was wound up and crazed. I didn't know when or how I could release my high level of energy; my treadmill wasn't there. I couldn't walk on the beach and leave Ava alone, so I paced around the room. Thank God Ava was oblivious to the state I was in.

I calmed a little after a couple hours, enough to sit down, at least. I reached for my cell phone and searched for Matty in the text messages. His name and my last text to him the morning of the accident came up. I reread: "Ditto." It felt a lifetime had passed since I wrote that message, but also as if it had happened yesterday. I felt uncomfortable and confused, as though I'd just awakened from a coma, I'd been told my husband was dead, and that he died two years ago, when I was sure I had talked to him yesterday. It's as though my brain was trying to block the past two years. I walked my mind back to the accident day and forced it to remember everything I'd experienced since. I was having a conversation with my memory and pushing it to recall a block of time. "Remember that day? And then the funeral? Yeah, that's right, you remember."

My brain responded with, "Yeah, I guess so. Okay … yeah, that happened. Oh … I remember that now; that was horrible."

I texted a message to Matt: "I miss you so much today."

* * *

August brought in what would have been our sixteenth wedding anniversary on the third. I spent a good part of the day at a bridal shower for Natasha, a great girl who used to babysit for Ava. I was initially hesitant to attend such an event on that day, but I woke up wanting to go, so I did. I had a nice time meeting her friends and family. In the evening I went out for sushi by myself and called it a night. I couldn't help thinking of the scene in *The Sixth Sense*, when the widow went out to dinner alone to the restaurant where her husband proposed. I wondered if Matt was with me at the table earlier, like her deceased husband was in the movie.

The month also marked the end to the two-year magazine subscriptions Matt purchased right before he flew out for the last time. That month, for the last time, I would walk them from the mailbox straight to the recycling bin.

I noticed that I was not afraid of the death of someone close to me anymore. Two years before I would panic every other time the phone rang, thinking it was news of someone's death. Eventually I felt more that if it happened, it happened. Death, I decided, is predetermined from birth. There's nothing I could do to stop it.

Gone also was my inability to picture a future date. What used to be a black hole in my mind had become a calendar month again. I could see about six months out, but not more than that.

* * *

I received a call from my OB/GYN office telling me that my recent breast MRI showed cell division on the left side, which meant the cells were dividing and multiplying. I was told to schedule a biopsy immediately, which I did for a Thursday mid-month. I felt oddly removed from the thought that I might have breast cancer. I cared, but not as much as one would think. I wanted to believe my casual attitude was because I was being logical, that if the results come back positive, I would be fine. I relied on the fact that the abnormality had been detected early and my survival chances were therefore very good. I was more afraid to acknowledge the whisper in my head that said, "I don't care if I survive. This is a perfect way to go, because it won't be my fault."

On Friday I called for the results and was told they wouldn't be back until Monday. *Note to self: never get a biopsy later than Wednesday, or you have to wait over the weekend for results.* Saturday arrived and I began to think more and more about the results. *Am I getting nervous?* On Sunday I was happy to have a distraction I had been looking forward to. A friend of a friend was flying into town for business and had invited me to join him for dinner. He's an incredibly nice guy that I'd gotten to know a bit over the previous year through phone conversations, because he was an expert in a field I needed advice in. I did meet him in person once about fifteen months earlier.

In the few hours leading up to dinner, I was becoming quite anxious. I couldn't determine if it was because I was having dinner with him or because of waiting for the biopsy results. *It can't be him; it's not a date, and he's very clear about being in a happy, long-term relationship.* The doorbell signaled his arrival. I opened the door and almost fell backward. He was tall, probably six feet five inches, and I had absolutely no memory of his height from our meeting the previous year. If you'd asked me to describe him, I would have said he was five eleven or maybe six feet. I desperately tried to hide my shock when I welcomed him inside.

Please don't misunderstand; I didn't have a problem with his height. What was upsetting me was that I had no recollection of such an obvious characteristic, which would be like forgetting someone was missing an ear. *Was I that big of a mess when I met him a year ago?*

I pulled myself together and we left for dinner. I enjoyed every minute, because the conversation was easy and interesting, and he was a gentleman. He did everything right. He told me his plan was to marry his girlfriend and start a family. Sadness washed over me. I remembered what it was like to be that girl, the girl who had a great guy who was in love with her and wanted to marry her and spend the rest of his life with her.

I tossed and turned all night, and I knew it was because I would find out if I had breast cancer the next day, but honestly, it was also because of my friend. He reminded me a great deal of someone I loved for a very long time. That weekend represented another pivotal point in my healing for two reasons. First, I was relieved to know I did care if I had cancer. I finally cared if I lived or died. Second, I needed to love again and I wanted to remarry. Not right then or even the next year, but someday.

The next day I was told I did not have cancer; however, the cells that were dividing needed to be removed to avoid any chance of becoming cancerous some day. I scheduled the procedure for a few weeks out. It was an outpatient surgery and the recovery was minimal.

33

The Third Year Without Matt
September 2012 – August 2013

On September 3, the two-year anniversary of Matt's death arrived. Oddly, it wasn't horrible. Neither was August 24, the two-year anniversary of seeing him for the last full day. The third fell on Labor Day that year, so Ava was home from school. We grilled out and swam. I didn't tell Ava the significance of the day, but I started a conversation about Matt. We giggled over funny stories and shared some memories.

She said, "I want a dad I can see and talk to."

Her words hit me like a cannon ball to my stomach. I cleared my throat and gathered my thoughts. "Yeah? I can see why you'd say that, Ava. I really miss being married too. Someday I'll get married again, but I think it's going to be a long time from now."

The next day, I cleaned the house and found myself pausing on every picture of Matt. I didn't know when I could ever take the photos down or put them in another place. I wiped the glass on each photo gently, as if my fingers were actually touching his face. I brought myself back to the time and place each picture was taken in an attempt to experience each memory again. I walked to his chest of drawers, smelled his signature bottle of cologne, and closed my eyes. I pretended he was standing beside me.

Later in the day I stopped at a gas station and heard a couple bickering. Their argument sounded trivial, and I wanted to scream, "Shut up! You don't have to be right. Let it go; that person could die tomorrow."

* * *

I started volunteering at Freedom Riders in the Orlando area. It offered hippotherapy: physical, occupational, and speech-language therapy using the characteristic movements of a horse. (*Hippos* is Greek for horse, so no, there were no hippopotamuses on the farm.) Freedom Riders catered to special-needs children, and my job was to turn the horses out to pasture, clean the stalls, and perform general upkeep of the barn. I was signed on for every Tuesday for five months. I grew up on a farm, so after minimal training, I worked on my own, for the most part. It felt good to perform some physical labor outside of cleaning my home. I enjoyed caring for large animals again, and I got to work with some great people. The volunteer opportunity caught my eye in a city magazine, so once again, I just showed up. It gave me a purpose and filled some hours that might otherwise be fraught with anxiety and self-pity. I was happy to have the time to give, because what everyone says about volunteering is true; it helped me as much as it helped others.

I continued to volunteer at the food store once a week too, and I picked up working in the church nursery one Sunday a month. I met a woman in the nursery who lost her teenage son years before. Of course it was painful and she missed him terribly, but she accepted the loss as God's will. She was an inspiration, because she held no anger or resentment. I agreed with her about God's will, but I knew I had not healed as much as she had. She'd had many more years to come to terms with her son's death, and the stark difference between us was joy. She glowed with sincere happiness, whereas my happiness came and went. When joy wasn't with me, I faked it, so most of it was insincere. *I bet she doesn't have anger attacks like I do. When did her bouts of depression end?* What I witnessed in her gave me hope, hope that true joy would return to me someday. I wanted to glow with a current of happiness coursing through me daily, like she did. After meeting her, I believed it would happen someday.

One Wednesday, I was at the food store and working with one of the full-time employees. We emptied a huge bin of candy and marked prices on it. She and I had talked a bit in passing, but never in depth, one-on-one. I was glad we were working together that day, because I wanted to get to know her better. We talked about a number of things and ended up discussing our daughters. I learned we were both single moms to only daughters. She mentioned offhandedly that her daughter's father passed away a few years ago, so the burden of raising her daughter was all on her. She said it wasn't his time to go, and sadness flashed on her face.

She continued about her daughter, as if she had not just dropped a bombshell. I didn't know if it was because she did not want to hear, "I'm so sorry," or if she took for granted others would not respond with a question if she kept talking. I was not the average listener, though, because I knew what she'd been through. I interrupted her and told her my husband also passed away unexpectedly, two years prior. I stopped working and looked at her when I said it, to indicate that I was there to listen if she wanted to talk about it.

She looked up slowly from the bag of candy in her hand and looked right back down. "Oh," she said and looked uncomfortable. She set the bag down, backed away, and said she needed to check on something. "Be back in a minute," she said cheerfully. She didn't come back. When I saw her in the weeks that followed, she smiled and said "Hello," but avoided me. I felt sad for her. She was filled with pain, and I wondered if she had someone to talk with about her loss. If not for the uncommon support of my friends, that would've been me.

* * *

"Momma, I wish Daddy had a twin, so I could see him," Ava said as I prepared lunch one October afternoon.

I didn't look up from the cutting board. I tried to imagine the agony of seeing an identical twin to him. It was hard enough for me to look at his mother, sometimes, because the resemblance broke my heart. *An identical twin? Are you crazy?*

I responded, "It'd be nice to see him again, huh? I wish we could too." I knew Ava wanted a father figure. She wanted someone to toss her on the bed fifty times or carry her on his shoulders. I did not have the physical strength to do it.

Later in the month was the 2012 Florida Writer's Association Annual Conference. It was my "sophomore year," and I decided to pay to talk with an agent. I didn't have any written work to pitch, but I wanted a professional opinion on my potential memoir.

A small conference room was set up with an agent in each corner. We aspiring writers were lined up on chairs in the hallway waiting for our names to be called. I was nervous knowing I had to tell the agent, a stranger, my story. *What if I start crying? What if I blubber through my allotted ten minutes while she stares at me?* My adrenaline raced and my heart pounded in my ears. I chewed the skin around my fingernails like an animal gnawing on a bone to reach the marrow. I considered canceling. *I don't care if I lose the fee I've paid. I can't sit here any longer. Why did I do this? I don't even have a chapter written. I'm going to look like an idiot. That's it; I'm leaving*, I decided. I stood to gather my things. At precisely the moment I did, my name was called to meet with Ann. *Shit. Now I can't leave. I'm the only person who stood up. Damn it!*

I closed my eyes, inhaled a deep breath, and held it for a count of four. I pushed my shoulders back, opened my eyes, and exhaled slowly. *F*** it.*

I entered the room with a big smile and confidence out of nowhere. I approached Ann and said with excitement, "This'll be the easiest pitch you'll hear all weekend."

She chuckled at my uncommon opening. "Really? Why is that?"

"Because I haven't even begun to write," I said as if it were a good thing. "I would like your opinion as to whether my story is viable."

"I'd be honored. What's it about?"

I steeled myself to talk about my loss. I immediately focused on the bridge of her nose so it appeared I was making eye contact. I'd mastered this tactic when I needed to talk about the most painful loss in my life. This strategy was the only way I could say what I needed to say. I would crumble if I saw a sad face or teary eyes. It may have made me look cross-eyed, but I didn't care.

Here goes nothing. "I cannot find a book that speaks to the physical and mental reactions to grief I endured following my husband's death. Everyone knows a griever will be sad, angry, and disoriented, but a detailed account of the level of depression and rage I endured has not been written. I intend to write a brutally honest testimony, no holds barred. Grievers need their feelings validated."

"I'm interested. I'd like your first three chapters," she said, handing me her card.

What? Is she kidding? Is this out of pity? I looked her in the eyes to read her expression. She didn't have a sad face, and she was not fighting back tears. She was all business. *Oh my gosh. She's serious.* I was flooded with happiness and fought not to sprint out of the room. *Did this just happen? It did. I'm going to do this. I need to do this.*

I'm supposed to do this.

I was eager for the conference to end so I could get home and write. I was baffled that an agent actually asked for the first three chapters of my memoir. I had never written anything longer than a short story, so I wasn't sure where to begin. I decided to start by typing up all my journal entries written following the tragedy. I ended up with a solid thirty pages, single-spaced. I was wound up and worked at a maniacal pace. I cut the pages of journal entries into countless strips and separated them into piles of what would be my chapters. I stopped after a number of frenzied hours and surveyed what I'd done. *What a mess.*

The individual heaps of paper strips looked like a field of gopher mounds. I couldn't imagine how I was going to turn the chaos into a memoir that represented everything I wanted it to. *I'm not a writer. I can't do this. Who do I think I am, talking with an agent? I've never published anything. What am I doing?*

I dropped into a chair and exhaled. I needed to wrap my head around the task. I challenged myself aloud with four questions, and answered them in my thoughts. "Why am I doing this?" *I'm doing this to honor Matt and the man he was. I'm doing this to preserve a part of Ava's and my history.*

"Define what will success look like." *Success will be creating a resource that can ease a fraction of the anguish a griever is living with every day. Success will be demonstrating what a typical day engulfed in grief looks and feels like. Success* will be to validate a fellow griever's pain, rage, sadness, and hopelessness.

"How many books do I need to sell to be successful?" *Five. One for Matt's mother, one for Matt's sister, one for Ava, and one for me. I trust the fifth will land in the hands of a person who needs it.*

"Can I open myself up to judgment, criticism, and perhaps ridicule?" *Yes. Bring it on.*

I got back to work. I gathered chapter one's mound of paper strips, secured them to cardboard, and began to type. As the words on each strip were woven into a new chapter, I tore the paper off the cardboard and threw it away, until they were all gone. I moved to chapter two and repeated the process.

I finished the first three chapters within a month and sent them to the agent. She promptly replied that my memoir was not a good fit for her, but encouraged me to continue writing. I felt disappointed, but I wasn't surprised. *What are the chances that my first submission be picked up by the first agent I send it to?* I considered using her response as an excuse to abandon my project. I kind of wanted to quit anyway.

I didn't know at the time that my venture would take as long as it did. Starting in October 2012, I thought I would be finished by late spring, about seven months later. It ended up taking more than twice as long. I finished in February 2014, sixteen months after I started writing. Progress was slow because writing was difficult, second only to dealing with Matt's death. Writing with complete honesty plunged me back to the most painful days of my life. It forced me to relive my darkest days over and over.

Many days I experienced shock again and my adrenaline raced, yet my extremities were so cold that my fingers could not type. I was again filled with rage and wanted to lash out at somebody, anybody. I cried for hours and could not focus. My head throbbed, I couldn't eat, and that elephant was back, sitting on my chest. *Why am I torturing myself? Am I a masochist? I don't have to write this book.* But the truth was that I did have to write it, because it needed to be written. I wanted to do it for Matt, Ava, and me. I wanted to write it for someone else in pain, because death and loss will always be a part of our world. We all experience loss and grief uniquely, but I felt a portion of the population would benefit from what I had to say.

* * *

In late October, Ava had a relapse. She was combative and insulting to me. Her first-grade teacher said she'd been impatient with other classmates. Ava spent the night at a friend's house, and her mother told me Ava tried to sneak sweets when she was asked not to. I grounded her from playdates and sleepovers for the weekend.

On Friday night she was playing on my computer. She yelled for me because she couldn't figure something out. I was unable to go to her immediately because I was in the middle of making her favorite dinner. A few minutes later I heard her pounding on my laptop. *Oh hell no.*

I sprinted to the office. "Stop it, Ava!"

She glared at me. "If you would come in here when I need you, I wouldn't be mad."

I took her hand, walked her to the sofa, and pulled her onto my lap. "What's going on, Ava? The nicer I am to you, the meaner you are to me."

She started to cry. "My brain and my heart miss Daddy so much, I'm mad at you."

I held her, rocked her, and told her I understood. I was impressed that she realized she was making me her punching bag to make herself feel better. She cried for four to five hours. I held and rocked her the entire time. *The hell with making dinner.*

"Will I ever stop crying, Momma?" Ava finally asked.

"Yes, you will. You just need to get it out of you, and you'll feel better. We still have many good days." I talked about the fun we'd been having together lately. I was not sure it was effective, though. She stopped crying momentarily but then started up again, wishing her father had been a part of the story. *I can't win, but I don't know what else to do.*

The next day she was still a little upset but was much better. I didn't want to sweep her feelings under the rug, so I brought up what happened the night before. "I still miss him so much too," I told her.

"Yeah, but you don't cry anymore."

"I sure do cry, Ava, just not as much, and it's usually late, after you've gone to bed. Remember, I used to cry all the time. Back then, you didn't cry very much. Maybe that's why you're crying now."

The next day was Sunday, and as we walked to the car after church, I said, "I was thinking about Daddy in church today when they talked about people going to heaven. I really miss him."

"That's because church is evil and it makes you miss people who died."

I stifled a chuckle at the thought of church being evil, but I could see where a child would think that, much like thinking a hospital was where people went to die. "Church is not evil, Ava. They just talk about things that are painful to help us understand why bad things happen. They want to make us feel better. It's always better to talk about what hurts you, so you can get it out of you. We haven't been to New Hope for a long time, Ava. Would you want to go back there again?"

She nodded "Yes."

* * *

As November rolled in, I called New Hope for Kids to ask if we could attend the two sessions that month. It would be good for me too, because I was anxious about the holidays, and writing my memoir was almost killing me.

On the day we were supposed to revisit New Hope, Ava told me she didn't want to go.

"They made room especially for us," I replied, "We need to go, but we never have to go again if you don't want to after today."

We walked into New Hope and got a warm welcome back. It was nice to catch up with people I hadn't seen for six months. They all seemed to be doing well and coping, although no one was looking forward to the holidays. I spied some new members, and I was sad that they'd just lost a loved one. *They've got a long haul ahead of them.*

Enduring Matt's death had given me a deep empathy for other grievers, and I tried to offer them some hope. I told them, "I'm just over two years out from my husband's death. I still have many bad days, but they aren't in an endless chain of days like they used to be. I still reach the depths of depression I once did, but it doesn't last as long as it used to. I am a Bobo doll in the grieving process. One of those dolls that is weighted at the bottom, and when you punch it, it keeps bouncing back up. Sometimes I'm down for days on end, and sometimes it's only an afternoon. I know when depression hits, you think you'll never get back up, but I promise, you will." I continued, "I'm not healed completely yet, and I don't think I ever really will be, but what was once a huge, gaping hole is now closing and scabbing over. One day it will scar, and that's the best it will ever be."

After the session ended I checked in with Ava. She was very animated and chatty. She told me the project for the day was to draw what she missed the most about her father. She drew Matt and her playing together and then stamped a big heart around them. She admitted she was glad we went and wanted to go next time too.

I wondered if she too recognized that she had come a long way in the last two years. I could see myself in the grievers with the freshest wounds. I knew I'd progressed, which brought a feeling of relief, but it was eclipsed with sadness for those new in their journey. I could see their pain on their faces and in their vacant eyes.

We went to New Hope for one more session, and it was the last time.

*   *   *

Ava and I flew up to Wisconsin for Thanksgiving and enjoyed time with our family. Holidays were easier in the moment, but they were still hard in the days leading up to them and then afterward. When we returned home, I couldn't return to writing. It was too hard.

Just before nine o'clock one morning, I was reading in a coffee shop and looked up to see a father with his little girl. He was gentle with her. I heard her say, "Let's go to school." She must have been four years old and in pre-K, because it started at nine. Watching him reminded me of how Matt was with Ava. She was that age when he died. They walked out the door and my eyes filled with tears.

A woman jolted me back to reality by asking if the seat next to me was taken. I turned quickly, and she saw my tears. She looked concerned and was about to ask me if I was okay.

"No one is sitting there, but you may hear me sneezing; my allergies are really bad right now." I smiled and pointed to my eyes. My lie worked.

*   *   *

December began with Ava and me participating in the Winter Park parade, walking with Freedom Riders to increase area awareness of the hippotherapy program. We helped dress the horses in holiday attire and covered the horse trailer in colorful wrapping paper. Ava and I were dressed for the season to hand out candy to parade watchers. Ava also wore a headband with a wire that arched up and around to dangle a piece of mistletoe a couple inches in front of her forehead. She was so adorable I could hardly stand it. This event became the highlight of our year. We had so much fun our faces were sore from smiling for the entire length of the parade.

A week later we saw *The Winter Wonderettes* musical production and had a fabulous time. Ava was called up on stage along with two other people from the audience. Each one was given an instrument and assigned a holiday word. They were instructed to make noise with their instrument every time the actresses sang their given word. Ava's word was *joy*, and she was handed a tambourine. She shook it about every third time she was supposed to, because she was giggling and unable to pay attention.

Those two events put us in the Christmas spirit, and I looked forward to the holiday much more than I thought I would. With each joyful event or day, though, there was a shadow of sadness because I was not sharing it with Matt. I sent out Christmas cards with a cute picture of Ava in a Santa hat. It killed me to omit Matt's name, so I didn't write any names. I signed it "The Bell Girls."

* * *

In mid-December, I agreed to a blind date. I was a bit excited a few days leading up to the lunch, but as it neared, I panicked. I wanted to cancel the date, but I also wanted to go and get it over with. As I dressed and applied makeup, I felt sickened by my own reflection. I felt guilt for wanting an unknown man to think I was pretty, for wanting his attention.

I arrived at the restaurant at the same time he did; I knew it was him because he looked exactly as he was described. He was attractive and gregarious. We found we had quite a bit in common, so the conversation was easy. He cracked a few jokes too, and I was happy to be enjoying myself. I was also fixated on the time, and as it passed, I thought, *Thirty minutes down, thirty to go.*

He asked me what I did for a living, and I told him I was a stay-at-home mom. "I've always wanted to be a writer too, so I've also been doing some writing lately."

"That's cool, what do you write?"

I replied with my rehearsed answer, "Short stories, and I have an idea for a kid's book."

"So you're not getting paid but you get to stay at home and write? Looks like I just hit the jackpot," he joked.

I laughed it off, but I was stunned. I knew he was joking and trying to be clever, but his remark was upsetting. I've always had to work, so a comment like his covered new ground for me. I was uncomfortable and at a loss for words. The sassy part of me thought, *You didn't hit anything, and trust me, you're not going to.* Instead I held a deep breath for a second and said, "Matt is still taking care of us."

The date ended on a good note and he asked if he could see me again. I said I might call, but it would be after the

New Year; the holidays were too busy. We said goodbye and left. I was ecstatic on the drive home. *I did it, and it wasn't terrible.* I knew I wasn't going to call him, but not because of anything he said. I honestly just wanted to see if I could get through a date. The poor guy had to be the sacrificial lamb. He was cute and funny though, so I was sure he would do just fine.

* * *

Christmas Eve arrived, and my brother, his family, and his in-laws all came to my house for dinner. We started with a champagne toast and appetizers. My brother helped by grilling the steaks while I put everything else together in the kitchen. The kids had their own menu, and their table was decorated for the holiday. We began with a prayer of joy and thanksgiving and then my sister-in-law Stacey added, "And we think of those we love who are not with us today. Amen."

I looked up and met her gaze, silently thanking her with a smile. It hit me that she did the same thing the previous year, but in my fog, I don't think I had acknowledged it. Now I realized that she did it not only because she loved Matt so much, but also because she was doing it for me. I still crumbled to speak of him at emotionally charged celebrations, because his absence remained hurtful. She said the words for me. *Thank you, Stacey.*

* * *

On New Year's Eve, we were included in our neighbors' annual party. Ava was determined to make it to the ball drop that year. She lay her head on my lap at 10:30 and said she was going to rest for a little bit. She fell asleep in seconds. With her head on me, I was captive on the sofa and didn't get the chance to leave early. I enjoyed great conversations with those around me, though, conversations I might not have had, which was yet another gift. Going home early would've been much easier, where I could get in my pajamas and open a bag of chips. *Could I be any lazier, considering the party is a forty-foot walk out my back door?* I really wanted to go home, because then I could avoid the part where I shared my marital status with the new people I met. My speech was becoming more rehearsed and less painful as time passed, but I loathed the look of pity in other people's eyes, and it happened every time. I knew that if the situation were reversed, I'd be the one with pity in my eyes for the person sharing such information. The response was instinctive, and then again, I'd probably be irritated if people didn't react with sympathy. It was a no-win situation.

* * *

Thursday, January, 10, the day before what would have been Matt's forty-first birthday, I wrote in my journal, "Today is a tough day. How is it possible that a man that great doesn't get to reach age forty-one? I'm pretty grumpy all day. It helps to clean. My house is very clean today."

On the next day, I wrote, "Today wasn't as bad as yesterday, but it's always worse leading up to an important date than the actual date. Trista and I took Kristy to lunch because she turned thirty-seven Wednesday. Ava and I then went to Dena's, so the girls could play. We ordered pizza. I'm just glad today is over."

* * *

At the end of the month I ordered a new sofa and loveseat to replace the worn set. A week later I bought a side table for the guest room and a tall plant stand to put in the entrance to the house. Making decisions on what furniture to buy wasn't hard that time, but I felt a pang of guilt for the changes I was making. It was uncomfortable to see transformations in our home. *If Matt walked in right now, he wouldn't recognize these things,* but of course, he's never going to walk in again.

Making changes was hard because it was a visible declaration that life moved on. My actions reflected a splitting off from the life I once led. I didn't want to forge a new path, but that's exactly what I was doing, almost subconsciously. It angered me, disappointed me, and yet was a relief to me.

* * *

On Valentine's Day I was happy to wake without heaviness. A feeling of joy was with me the entire day, and I could only believe it was coming from prayers being said for my benefit. I couldn't imagine being able to be as happy all day through my own accord.

My forty-second birthday was later that month and highlighted by attending a P!NK concert as well as a number of lunches and dinners with friends. I hadn't written for three months, and it felt great not to be reliving the pain. I considered stopping altogether, because it was nice to separate myself from it.

I had been reading Bible stories to Ava from a book geared toward children. It told about women in the Bible and the strength they showed in times of adversity. I didn't think to censor it for content. One of the stories was about a husband who died and was brought back to life by Jesus. The story was a bit upsetting to me, and I knew it must have been hard for Ava to understand. I knew she was wondering why Jesus didn't bring her father back to life.

We said our prayers, and I asked her what she was thinking about.

"I'm a little mad at God for taking Dad away."

"Okay. I understand that."

"Why didn't he send him back to us?"

"I don't know, Ava. I wish he would have too, but he didn't. I get angry with God sometimes too. We lost someone we loved, and since God makes everything happen, of course we're going to be angry with him. It's normal; God knows that. It's okay to be angry with God a little bit, but don't let it last. When you are angry with God, talk to him. Ask him to make you feel better."

* * *

On Sunday, March 3, 2013, Ava and I went to church and to Panera Bread afterward. As we ate I was distracted, thinking the day was the two-and-a-half-year mark of Matt's death. It seemed as if it was only a couple months before, because the pain was so fresh some days. I heard a girl band playing "Boys of Summer" in the background. Matt knew this song was my all-time favorite. I wondered if he had anything to do with the song selection. When we left the restaurant and sat in the car, both Ava's and my seat belts locked up.

The end of March marked two events; Ava turned seven, and I was sent the Order of Discharge of Matt's estate. The document was signed by a judge and officially released me of any further responsibility or liability in connection with his estate. Matt missed three of Ava's birthday parties, and another piece of his life was chipped away.

* * *

On April 5 , I wore my ear buds as I cleaned closets, drawers, and cubbyholes. My thoughts were saturated in Matt; he was all I could think about. I recalled our entire life together: meeting him, moving to Florida, traveling, and Ava's birth. I turned over and over our best memories together and relished them. I thought of September 3, 2010, and what I could remember of what had happened since. I had to keep reminding myself that the tragedy really happened; he was really dead. I said aloud, "Okay, I get it, he's gone." I was filled with a feeling of defeat. I felt like I had been fighting a fight I could never win, except I just figured it out after going fifty rounds. An acceptance came over me, much like it did in April two years earlier, but on a distinctively deeper level.

My iPod was playing "Snow" by Sleeping At Last. The song was beautiful yet haunting, about a cold day in December. It speaks of the greatness and joy of the season, yet refers to the extreme pain resulting from loss that surfaces during the holiday.

The song hit me like a boulder. Whoever wrote it knew the pain of loss. Holidays, especially Christmas, had become so bittersweet. The words were an encouragement to accept our loss, and although a person is gone and can never be replaced, we simply must move on. We must find solace in others who share our loss. We must let go of what once was and accept what we have now.

I sat on the floor, leaned against the wall, and listened to the lyrics, and I finally let go. I mentally stepped into the next phase of my life. *It's time to revise.* I knew I was letting go of my previous life, and I faced the challenge of embracing my new life, my after-Matt life. I sat with my head in my hands and wept. Tears rolled down my immobile face coupled with shallow, quiet breathing. Even my crying had changed. Gone was the violent wailing with red, swollen eyes stung by hot tears. My sinuses were not swollen, congesting my face. I did not breathe heavily, trying to catch my breath. The fight was gone, even in how I expressed emotion. No headache followed; no recovery was necessary.

I stood up to continue cleaning. In the linen closet I happened across a gift I'd bought for Ava months earlier. *Oops, forgot about that one.* It was a small decorative pillow embroidered with the words, "She held her head high and stepped into her latest adventure." I decided the pillow was actually the perfect gift for me. I kept it to mark that day, my Day of Acceptance.

I was unaware of the song that played after "Snow," but "Kite" by U2 came on. My interpretation of the song is that it's the words from a person who has passed. He's confused at what has just happened, but he seems to understand that his own death was meant to be. The person is singing to the one he left behind and encouraging her to go on. He doesn't want her to spend her life being sad. He assures her he will see her again.

"Kite" was one of four songs played at Matt's funeral. I had heard it play on my iPod many times since then. Each time before today, whenever I heard Bono sing "I want you to know that you don't need me anymore," it felt like Matt singing right to me. I would argue in my head, *Yes, I do, Matt. I do need you.* That day it was different. Deep inside me, begrudgingly I acknowledged, *You're right, Matt. I don't need you anymore.* It was the end of Dawn and Matt. It was the end of a commitment so powerful that it could have ended only in death. The realization broke my heart and a tidal wave of despair enveloped me.

To believe and accept that I didn't need Matt was a frightening realization. I wanted to need him. I enjoyed needing him. In Matt I knew I had absolute, unfaltering support to withstand anything the world threw at me. Now he was gone. I was alone.

It was crucial to my healing to accept that I didn't need Matt. I still missed him, I still wanted him, and I still loved him, but I didn't need him. To realize that I didn't need him was the first step toward diminishing my want for him. When you don't need an object or a person in your life, you don't want that object or person in you life as much as you thought you did.

Need for the deceased is the first emotion to go. Want for the deceased is the second emotion to go. True love for the deceased, defined as agape, will never go away. Eros, passionate love with sensual desire and longing, must go away, or a griever will never be able to fully move on to a new lover.

* * *

The second week of April, I returned to my memoir. It had been a blissful break since Thanksgiving, but I had a nagging desire to finish it. I read all that I had written to that point and cried so much I was not sure I would stop. The next few months were a roller coaster of emotions because I dredged up the pain I had tried to pretend was over. From the outside, you would probably never have guessed I was still in the grieving process, that it was still intense. It had been almost three years since the accident so you'd likely chalk up my irritability and withdrawal to the fact that I was having a bad day. On my most grieving days I isolated myself, not only because I didn't want to be ugly to everyone around me, but also because I didn't want to admit to myself that I was still grieving. I still held great pain inside of me. Here are a few of my journal entries:

April 11: I'm all over the place. I can smile and laugh with someone one minute and fight back tears the next.

April 13: I'm a mess and am ungracious company. It takes very little to set me off.

April 19: Was supposed to write but couldn't. Angry and weepy again.

April 22: Became enraged talking with a friend over a controversial topic and could not shake my anger. My mind is going in circles, untamable, and I'm spitting nails at everyone.

April 24: I know I'm writing all day tomorrow, and I've felt heaviness and fear all week, trying to prepare myself.

April 25: I wrote all day today. I feel like I was hit in the head with a wrecking ball and then made to run a marathon. I'm truly mentally, physically, and emotionally exhausted, and I've not even written much.

* * *

One Sunday Ava and I went to brunch after church. A physician assistant I used to call on as a sales representative walked by with his family. He was a great guy and I smiled at seeing him, but he didn't see me. I was reminded that the last time I saw him, I was in my old life.

Ava and I finished our meals, and I walked over to his table to say hello and introduce Ava. The PA smiled and seemed happy to see me too. He introduced his wife, his parents, and a couple siblings. I introduced Ava to them, and we chatted for a bit. I walked away and felt my stomach turn. I imagined he was telling them how he knew me. He was probably identifying me as Dawn, the rep whose husband died. I was not just Dawn anymore; I was Dawn whose husband died.

* * *

On the day after Mother's Day, I woke in a deep depression. I felt it coming on the day before and was now fidgety and irritated. I couldn't do anything productive, and I was glad Ava was in school. I lay on the sofa for hours and stared at the wall. I missed Matt immensely and feared I would always be alone. I had been on three more blind dates since the first one in December, and I didn't want to go on a second date with any of them. *I'm ruined for any other man.*

The depression lingered through the next day, but instead of lying down, I forced myself to stay busy around the house. I was angry and negative and declared it an NPD-No Phone Day. I noticed a shift had occurred. Before, the days leading up to a special day or event were the hardest; now it was harder afterward. I seemed to have the strength to reach the day and survive it, but when it was over, I crashed.

* * *

On Thursday, May 23, Ava came home from school upset. She told me some of her classmates were asking how her father died.

She said, "I told them his plane crashed into the side of a mountain. They just kept staring at me."

Ava knew his plane crashed into the ground, not into the side of a mountain, so I was curious as to why she changed the facts, but it was not worth discussing at the moment.

"Ava, they weren't trying to be mean. They just wanted to know. If someone told you her dad or even her dog died, you'd want to know how it happened, don't you think?"

She looked at the floor and nodded slowly. I continued, "People ask me too, all the time. It's the first question they ask when I tell them my husband died, but the people who ask me are older, so they know they're not supposed to stare at me. Kids don't know that, Ava. They don't know what else to do."

We left the next day to spend Memorial Day weekend in Wisconsin. She had only a day and a half left of school when we returned, so I didn't contact her teacher regarding the kids' questions.

During our visit in Wisconsin, we decided to go to Matt's grave for the first time. We were going to bring a dozen red roses and a hot dog, because he loved both. The only time I'd been to the cemetery was when I chose which plots to buy and then attended the interment. I didn't drive either time, but I assumed I'd find the cemetery easily. I should have known better. I had been so worked up all week leading up to that day that I couldn't think straight. I confused the highway I needed with another one that ran parallel to it, so I was driving in circles. I was frustrated because it was getting late and the sun would set soon. I was angry and I spun myself into a full-on tantrum, yelling, swearing, and driving erratically. *Ah, another proud day for Dawn.*

I finally found the cemetery, parked, and walked to the gravesite. I looked at the headstone and shook my head. Ava was walking behind me.

I knelt to her level and touched her arm. "This is where your father is buried. Do you remember the day that we came here, after we were in the church?"

She looked at me with big, sad eyes and nodded.

"Do you want to give these to him?" I asked, offering the flowers and hot dog.

She nodded again. She dropped to her knees and put them down just under the headstone. Her tiny hands ran across the engraving, and she started to weep.

"Do you want me to walk over by that tree, so you can talk to him?"

"Yes."

I walked to the tree and turned to watch her. There was nothing I wanted to say at his gravesite, because I didn't believe he was there, in the ground. I have always felt him with me, so the visit to a field in Wisconsin was insignificant to me.

Ava crumbled. She spoke and cried loudly, but I could hear only pieces of what she was saying. Some of it was angry. It was killing me not to run over to her, but she needed to be in the moment on her own. When her hysteria ebbed, I walked to her and rubbed her back. I saw a spot of blood on one of her hands and could tell she had picked off the skin around her thumbs. *Like mother, like daughter.*

She fell into me sobbing and wailed, "Why did he have to die? Why? Why? Why?"

I held her and said, "I don't know, Ava. I don't know."

We sat in each other's arms for maybe fifteen minutes. The sun had set behind the trees and the air was getting chilly. I told Ava we needed to go. I led her to the car.

I was livid. I wanted to know why he died too. Between writing, getting lost, and now seeing my precious, innocent child in such pain, I couldn't control myself. *Well, God, why don't you just come down here and tell us why? Then we'd both f***ing know! But you're not going to, are you? Just let those Bell girls figure it out themselves.*

I drove forty minutes to my parents' house, and Ava sobbed most of the way. She kept repeating "Why?" with her eyes closed. She finally fell asleep from emotional exhaustion. I calmed down with deep, relaxing breaths. *I'm sorry, God. I know everything is all in your plan, but it sure hurts.*

* * *

May 30 was the final day of first grade for Ava, and also the day I met with her teacher to get her results from the gifted program testing. Mrs. Roney told me Ava's scores were high and she qualified for the program. The results helped explain why Ava had been so frustrated at school. She needed to be more challenged throughout the day.

I found the perfect school with a curriculum that taught one grade level above the current grade, and the students moved as a group to each class throughout the day. I decided that the academics would challenge her and the constant movement would stimulate her. Ava and I went on a tour, she was screened for admission, and I enrolled her to begin second grade the following August. The only downfall to the school was the location. It was a twenty-five-minute drive with no traffic, but our commute time would require us to battle traffic every morning, causing the one-way travel time to almost double.

The school was close to an area I'd always wanted to live. It was adorable with many boutique shops and outdoor restaurants and a large park, and it offered numerous activities such as movies in the park and holiday parades. *Can I move? Can I leave the home that Matt bought for us? The last home he lived in?* Moving was a big decision that could not be made lightly. I spoke with Ava, my friends, and my mother-in-law about it to get their input. Everyone was supportive and said it would be a great new start for Ava and me. I agreed with them, but I felt a pang of guilt at the thought of leaving our home.

* * *

In mid June I was faced with a number of home maintenance issues. My security system was acting up again, the sprinklers weren't spraying all the zones, and only one room in the entire home had a landline working. At least it was the office, so my fax machine worked. Additionally, my Internet service was knocked out. After many customer service calls, a technician determined that my router was shot. I bought a new one, plugged in the tutorial CD, and took a deep breath. Technical efforts were not my strength. The venture was equivalent to a non-runner lining up for a marathon. Somehow I did it.

Because of all the maintenance and upkeep issues at my house, I decided it was okay for us to move. A condo would be ideal, so home maintenance was minimal. I ambled around my home and imagined leaving it for the last time. As I entered each room, I was flooded with memories of our moving in more than five years before.

I stepped out to the lanai and pool. This area was the only place I ever pictured Matt. During the afternoons of his two-week breaks, he loved to be in the hot tub with his arms crossed on one edge, watching CNN. I'd always teased him because he looked like a frog with his head poking out of the water. The decision to move settled in me, knowing Matt was not attached to the house, and he would always be with us.

* * *

Well into June, Ava and I were enjoying the summer. One day she was cleaning her room and dancing around to music. She used my old iPhone as an iPod, and I'd downloaded lots of pop music and soundtracks from kids' movies. I was in the next room and smiled as I listened to her belting out the words to the songs on speakerphone. I pictured her with a hairbrush microphone. After a couple minutes, I realized I couldn't hear her singing anymore. I listened to the music and heard a song that seemed to be on repeat. My stomach fell, because it was one that was played at her father's funeral.

I quietly approached her bedroom, and from the hallway, I heard her sobbing. I said nothing as I curled up behind her on the bed and rubbed her arm. She cried for at least an hour as we listened to the song play over and over. We both dozed off. When we awoke I asked, "Do you want to talk about anything?"

"No."

"Do you want to get a movie and a pizza?"

"Yes."

* * *

On a Sunday in mid July, we walked into church in a great mood. I saw a lot of people I knew and was chatting and waving as if I were running for office.

The prelude signaled everyone to sit down. It was a classical piece familiar to me, and it brought a smile to my face. *Where do I know this from?* I remembered with a jolt, it was Pachelbel's "Canon in D," the same prelude we chose for our wedding. Tears immediately filled my eyes. I pinched between them to make it stop. I was blue the rest of the day.

* * *

August 3, what would have been our seventeenth wedding anniversary, I was sullen, but not terribly. I bought myself a dozen white roses and enjoyed a quiet evening with Ava. I spent some time looking at condos for sale and imagining a fresh start.

A week later Ava invited a friend over and the girls were playing in her toy room. I checked on them and saw that one of the stuffed animals was on Ava's desk with a small blanket covering it.

"What are you guys up to?" I asked.

"Oh, the elephant died, so we're having a funeral," Ava said matter-of-factly.

Wonderful. "Okay, umm, how did it die?" I asked, forcing myself to not freak out.

"It was just old," Ava's friend said.

Neither one of them seemed upset, so I let it go. "Okay, let me know when you're ready for lunch," I said as I walked away.

I followed up later in the day and asked Ava if she had fun with her friend. She said yes.

"How did the funeral go?" I asked.

"What? Oh yeah, it was fine, but we didn't really bury him. He's back on my chair," she said.

I assumed this play behavior was normal, and she wasn't upset, so I ended my questioning. I was not sure if the incident reflected healing for her or not, but I hoped so.

In mid August I awoke around eleven o'clock at night to the sound of my home alarm going off. I was panic-stricken. *Someone's trying to break in.* I bolted out of bed to the keypad. It reported that a pool door had been opened. I have three doors leading to the pool. I checked to see that they were all still closed and locked. I shut off the alarm and turned on the outdoor lights. Nothing. It came to mind that I did not hear a screen door slam when the alarm went off. There were two screen doors off of the pool cage, and if someone came in through there and tried to open a door to the house, he'd have to run out through the same screen door when he heard the alarm sound. I couldn't imagine anyone would take the time to close it quietly. I looked outside and noted that the screen doors weren't propped open either. *How odd.*

I reset the alarm and went back to bed. I was dozing off when the alarm sounded again. The keypad reported the same message. I repeated all my previous steps. I wasn't sure what was setting off the alarm, but it was not a burglar. To avoid a three-peat, I left the alarm off and returned to bed.

I fell asleep, and in my dream I was speaking with Matt. *Finally.* He was irritated and rambling on at the incompetence of the security company. "You should never be afraid in this house. I'm telling you, Dawn, it's nothing; it's just the sensors. They're not lined up, and it's causing the alarm to trip."

I woke up and replayed the dream. I chuckled to myself at remembering how angry Matt used to get when someone didn't do a job well. Matt was meticulous in his work, and he expected the same of others. I called the security company and explained about the alarm tripping. The dispatcher told me a technician would be at my home in the morning.

The next day a technician came to my home and looked at the pool doors. I recounted the situation with the alarm going off and then left him to do his job. He found me in the kitchen a few minutes later and repeated almost exactly Matt's words from my dream. "It's nothing; it's just the sensors. They're not lined up, and it set the alarm off. I'll have them fixed in a few minutes." I couldn't speak, I only nodded that I understood.

* * *

At the end of August, the General Civil Aviation Authority released the final report regarding Matt's plane crash. The GCAA is to the United Arab Emirates what the National Transportation and Safety Board is to the U.S. The report was a 300-plus-page document describing the flight in detail from beginning to end. Much of it was technical and over my head, but I understood the gist of it. The cockpit voice recorder transcripts were included and the thought of reading them terrified me. I'd been tortured over the past three years believing the last twenty-eight minutes of Matt's life were filled with sheer terror, knowing the flight was doomed. I agonized over reading his words, hearing him full of fear. Not a day had gone by without my thinking of it, and it had affected every corner of my life.

I took Ava to school and returned home to read the report. It stated verbatim on page 128,

> The time interval between take off and the data ending was 51 minutes, the fire bell sounding and there was smoke detected in the cockpit before the Uncontrolled Flight into Terrain (UNCIT) was approximately 29 minutes; the time from the fire bell to the Captain oxygen supply stopping abruptly was 5 minutes 30 seconds; the Captain left his seat 8 minutes after the fire bell.

The captain went to look for oxygen and sadly never returned, which left Matt, the FO, first officer, as now the PF, pilot flying, alone in the cockpit for twenty-four minutes and thirty seconds until the plane made contact with the ground. Page 136 reads verbatim,

> Judging by the transmissions, the PF has very limited information ... the PF can judge what has been demanded but not the response. There are several references to the smoke in the cockpit, the inability to view inside or outside the cockpit, the increasing heat, lack of oxygen supply and that the PF cannot see the primary flight displays speed or altitude indicators.

I read the radio transcripts, and I was filled with pride and amazement at how professional Matt was as he fought to land the plane. He was composed and confident in his words and actions the entire time.

What was not recorded were any messages or last words to Ava or me, a fact that told me he did not know how dire his situation was. If he had known, he would have said final words to one or both of us; that's the kind of man he was. Realizing that he did not know he was doomed brought me immeasurable relief. Peace flowed through me, and that night I slept like I had not slept in three years.

34

Three Years to Present Without Matt
September 2013 – February 2014

September 3 marked the three-year anniversary of Matt's death. It was a Tuesday, so Ava was in school. My plan was to write all day, but I couldn't. I was grumpy, so I ran it out of me on the treadmill, organized a closet, and watched an episode of *Revenge* I had recorded.

* * *

A week later, I picked Ava up from school, and after she climbed into the back seat, she told me she had a bad day. She asked one of her teachers something and was told a couple times to have her father go online.

Ava told me, "She kept saying 'Ask your dad,' so I finally said I didn't have a dad."

"Okay. What did your teacher say then?"

"She didn't say anything, and then class was over and a couple other kids started asking me why I didn't have a dad."

"What did you say?"

"Nothing. I just walked away, but one of the girls said, 'Of course she has a dad; he's just not here.'"

A similar situation had happened the previous May. Last time she was asked this question, she said her father died in a plane crash, but she was in a new school for second grade, with all new teachers and classmates.

I gave her the same response I did in May. "Ava, they are not being mean or trying to hurt your feelings when they ask about your dad. They are just curious. I know it's hard, but if you just look them in the eye and tell them he died in a plane crash, they'll stop asking."

Irritation swelled in me. I hated that my little girl had to deal with a situation that was so unfair to a seven-year-old. I wouldn't allow her to feel ashamed or inferior to anyone because of it. "And you say it like that's just the way it is. You keep looking them in the eye and say 'Any more questions?'" I said with a little attitude.

I continued, "Ava, I get asked these questions, and they make me sad too. I want you to know that the fact that your father has passed away does not mean you should feel embarrassed about it. It happened. It's horrible, but it happened, and now you are a little girl whose father died and I am a woman whose husband died. That's just the way it is, and you need to practice how you answer questions about your dad so you have to answer them only once. Our home is not like everyone else's home, but our home is still happy. Got it?" I looked in the rearview mirror and saw her nodding.

* * *

In mid September my goal was to introduce and market myself as a writer. I needed a logo, a Facebook business page, a Twitter account, a personal website, and business cards. I did not have the skills to do these things myself, but I was fortunate to be introduced to someone who could help me, Anthony Fernandez of Tony Enterprises. Anthony did an exceptional job creating my social platform, and everything was complete and ready to launch within two weeks. It all happened fast, and it scared me. I stalled Anthony while I wrestled with what to do.

As much as I wanted to announce what I was doing, I was afraid to do it. Once I took that step, there was no going back. I was afraid to open myself up to judgment and criticism. I also faced the fear of failure. I became increasingly insecure about my writing ability. *What if I'm the American Idol hopeful who thinks she can sing, but she really can't? What if everyone in the country knows it but me? Am I that girl?*

I kept vacillating between being completely confident with my work and being struck down with paralyzing anxiety. Many days I wanted to trash everything I had written. The only thing that kept me on track was the encouragement of my friends. I confessed my fears to them. "I feel like I'm a bride on the day before her wedding, and I'm not sure I want to marry the guy. It's my last chance to stop everything before it's too late."

I also reached out to my mother-in-law for advice. She said, "You're on the edge of a cliff right now. Just jump."

So I did. I gave Anthony the go-ahead, and my social platform launched. It was not as painful as I thought it would be. Now I had to ask people to Like my page and follow me on Twitter. It was uncomfortable because I did not like asking people to do things for me, but I did it. All I could do was ask them, and people either did or they didn't.

An unexpected joy was the number of people I had never met who reached out to me through my website. They sent me direct messages about losses they had endured, some that happened recently. I was honored by the opportunity to send them some advice. Through the website, Twitter, and Facebook, I received countless notes of encouragement and support from friends, family, and strangers. To say I was humbled would be an understatement.

Thank you, Anthony.

I reached out to my friend Kymi Swanepoel, who lived in South Africa. We used to work together in Wisconsin. She always had a flair for art and graphic design, so I asked her to design my book cover. We e-mailed back and forth until we settled on one with a picture of a three-diamond wedding band against a black background. It was perfect, and I couldn't be happier with her work.

I asked her how she knew the wedding ring she chose was identical to mine. Matt gave it to me five years before, and I had not seen her in that time. Oddly enough, she chose it randomly from clip art. *Thank you, Kymi.*

* * *

In mid October Ava and I flew up to Wisconsin for a family reunion. We decided to visit Matt's gravesite again. It was much smoother that time, mostly because I didn't get lost. Ava again wanted a few minutes alone, so I retreated to the same tree where I had stood the previous May. She was clearly sad as she spoke to him, but did not wail or rip the skin off her thumbs.

The weekend after we flew back was the annual Florida Writer's Association convention. That year was my third and much more fun, because I knew all the people from the writer's critique group I joined the year before. I again paid a fee to talk to a literary agent. In contrast to the previous year, I had a strong start to my memoir and had launched my social platform.

I met with an agent out of California who represented memoirs. I gave him my pitch, and he clearly was not impressed. "You're really at the very beginning stages of your memoir," he said. "You've got a long way to go. And you have a social platform, but you just launched it. You really need to expand on both fronts, and maybe you'll be ready next year."

Ouch. Okay then. Um ... Thank you? I was definitely disappointed with his feedback, but it did not deter me. I had a good story to tell, a testimony to give. I may not be the most gifted writer, but I trusted that my words would help someone.

* * *

I decided it was time to reach out to all the people who clicked Like on Matt's Facebook page that originated immediately after his death. I asked Pete to give me admin rights, and he did within minutes. On October 26 I logged on to the Facebook page and looked over all the kind messages that had been sent over the past three years, not only to Matt, but also to our family. I wrote the following message to everyone from me:

Hello Everyone,

This is Dawn Bell, the woman lucky enough to have been married to Matt for fourteen years. It's been just over three years since the tragic accident, and I'm just now getting back on Facebook. I kept meaning to post on this site many times, but I just couldn't do it. Please forgive my absence.

I'd like to first thank Pete Dascoulias for creating this page immediately after receiving the news of Matt's death. It was integral in keeping everyone up to date on what was happening. Without your initiative and the reach of social media, many people would not have known when the repatriation and the funeral were scheduled. Thanks also for giving me admin rights to this page so I could post this message to all of you. For all you've done, Pete, I am sincerely grateful.

I also thank all of you who Liked this page. Whatever capacity it was that brought you here, be it a family member, friend, fraternity brother, fellow pilot, or otherwise, you came here out of respect and concern and perhaps love for him. I know Matt would be humbled by this honor you have shown him.

Our daughter Ava is seven now and has handled this loss as well as a child could. She is a strong and beautiful girl and is the spitting image of her father. I know Matt is looking down on her with joy and pride.

I am doing well also. I try each day to fulfill the promise I made to him at his funeral, to honor his memory by being thankful for the years we had him and not be angered by the years we will not.

Please join me today in a taking a moment to consider all the blessings in our lives.

Dawn

I hesitated before I sent it. I was very nervous, and swallowing became difficult. *Should I post this? Who am I to assume anyone wants to hear from me? What if Matt's picture pops up on someone's News Feed and upsets somebody?* I took a deep breath and clicked Post. I almost vomited.

Within sixteen minutes 333 people saw it, and the comments started to roll in. The messages of love, encouragement, and gratitude I received over the next five days were extraordinary. People that I haven't seen or spoken to in years wrote to me. Many people I had never met and would never meet wrote to me. In the end, 11,252 people representing thirty-three countries and nine languages saw the post. A total of 600 people Liked the post, fifty-seven wrote comments, and eleven people shared it. Without the power of social media, I would never have had the ability to reach that many people, and in hours. I still shake my head in awe of the technology available to us today that can be used for such an extremely personal need.

* * *

In early November my brother Ashley called to tell me he was speaking to a group of people at Celebrate Recovery in a few days. He planned to emphasize gratitude and asked if I had anything I could share from my book. I had yet to write the chapter on gratitude, but I wanted to send him something. Gratitude was imperative to my healing. I stopped everything I was doing and wrote a quick essay for him to use:

How did I survive the loss of my husband? In a nutshell, I had these three reasons:

1. Ava
2. Faith
3. Gratitude

When Matt Bell died unexpectedly in a plane crash on September 3, 2010, he left our four-year-old daughter Ava and me behind. Many mornings in the depths of grief I would never have gotten out of bed, were it not for my love for Ava. She is the reason I did not turn to excessive alcohol or anti-depression medications. She is the reason I didn't give in to the warming call of anger and self-pity. Trust me, I wanted to. It feels better to be angry than to be sad. It's easier to justify self-pity than it is to refuse it and humbly accept God's will.

I returned to God after my husband's death. I had never stopped believing in him but had stopped going to church and hearing his words for two decades. I'd grown undisciplined and lazy in my devotion. I knew I couldn't make it without God. I needed his help, help I could get only from him. I knew that if I didn't let God help me, the devil would help himself.

I did not harbor anger toward God, but I was very angry at not knowing the answers to my questions. "Why would you take away a man like Matt? Why would you leave Ava fatherless? What is the lesson in this tragedy? What good could possibly come of this?" It would have been easier to face and accept the loss if I knew *why*. I begged for answers. I demanded answers.

God does not work the way we want, however, and we all know it. The Lord gives and the Lord takes away. We usually will not learn the intention behind the lesson for years. Sometimes we'll not understand until our own death and return to God.

The power of gratitude is immeasurable. Being aware of all the gifts God has given us will fortify our spirits if God chooses to take those gifts away. Gratitude worked for me. On my darkest days I would recite a list of all the blessings I'd been given in my life. I had much to be grateful for, even in the wake of Matt's death. We've all heard that when you're laughing, you can't cry. I'll add that when you're grateful, you can't be angry.

Entitlement is the opposite of gratefulness. Understand that we are not entitled to a loving family, loyal friends, good health, talents, or possessions. These things too are gifts. Recognize them and be thankful for them. When we expect gifts to be given but not taken away, our hearts will be filled with resentment after a loss. We will fall prey to the dark side of our personalities, and our worst selves will emerge. Know that you are stronger than that.

Be grateful to God. Be humble. Expect less. Give more.

* * *

Thanksgiving arrived and instead of flying to Wisconsin, we stayed in town. It was a great day that started with hopping from a couple of neighbors' gatherings. We met extended families of our friends and got to nibble on appetizers. We then went to my cousin's home on Matt's side for a family dinner. The entire day and weekend couldn't have been any more enjoyable.

On December first, I started early and decorated the entire house. I enjoyed it and felt only a tinge of sadness when I put Matt's childhood ornaments on the tree. Ava and I attended many events throughout the month: a tree lighting downtown, festive meals with friends, and the Radio City Music Hall Rockettes Christmas Spectacular touring in Tampa.

I ordered Christmas cards with a picture of the two of us signed *The Bell Girls, 2013.* This card was the first time my picture had been on the annual card, and it was a strategic decision. Ava and I both had big smiles and looked genuinely happy. I ordered and sent out more than usual to announce that we were okay.

That Christmas was our third without Matt, and it was by far the most bearable. I did feel myself getting grumpier as we got closer to the twenty-fifth, but I was not grumpy with others, only when I was alone. The hardest moment that season was in church during Christmas Eve services. I was not sure why, probably because everyone around us seemed to be seated amid their complete families.

I was also struggling to finish my memoir. I was still oscillating between being fully on board to wanting to throw in the towel. The initial deadline I set was the end of the year, but I had stopped writing in the first part of December, rendering the deadline impossible. I didn't push myself because I wanted the finished product to be the best it could be, and I needed to be in the right frame of mind to do it. My friends encouraged me to stay the course and remember why I was doing it.

Christmas morning I woke early and waited four hours for Ava to awake. *Isn't this backwards?* We had fun opening our presents. Matt's mother sent some fabric snowballs, so we of course had to run around the house having a snowball fight. It was a good morning, and in the afternoon we joined my friend Cindy Hudson and her family for a holiday meal and great conversation.

* * *

On New Year's Eve Ava finally stayed awake long enough to witness her first countdown. We gave each other a big hug and a kiss, and then Ava said, "Can we go to bed now?"

Ten days later I finally got back to writing. I'd taken a month off, so I set a new deadline of January 31. The next day was Matt's birthday, and he would have turned forty-two. I bought a dozen red roses for the table and four purple balloons.

Ava and I each took two balloons and decorated them. I wrote a letter to him on one of my balloons. Ava asked me to read it; I did, and I fell apart.

We biked to an open field to release the balloons. Ava asked if I'd bring my cell phone so we could play a song from his funeral while we did it, and I did. She walked off to be alone for a few minutes to talk to her father. She returned and we freed our balloons and watched them rise until they disappeared.

At night we went to Matt's favorite restaurant for dinner. That day and the month weren't too painful, except for the birthday balloons. The last two Januarys, I had been incredibly angry. It was comforting to see progression in both of us.

* * *

We had toured a number of new homes for sale over the previous six months. I liked having Ava witness the entire process, and I explained negotiating, making an offer, counteroffers, inspections, and walk-throughs to her. I didn't want her ever to feel intimidated in buying a home as a single woman.

We finally found the ideal place, and I told Ava I was going to make an offer as soon as I dropped her off for school. We both loved it and were very excited. The first question she asked when I picked her up from school was, "Did they counter?"

I laughed to myself with a bit of pride, *Wow, she really does understand how the system works.* "They did, but then I countered, and they accepted, so … it's ours!"

She squealed with excitement and gave me a fist bump.

Ava didn't have school on February 14, which happened to be the closing date. Ava joined me to observe the closing, and we were handed the keys, not a bad Valentine's Day for us. I felt a flutter of wistfulness when I thought again about leaving the home we shared with Matt, but I knew it was time to step into our next chapter, and he would remain with us.

When we returned home I had flowers and chocolate waiting for her. I opened the decorated cards she made for me and saw that she also made a card for Matt.

Dear Daddy,

I hope you have a great Valentine's Day up in heaven. I miss you very, very much. I'll never, ever, ever forget you ever. I'll love you til even when I'm in heaven. This is for you forever and always.

Love,
Ava

I was beaming with pride for her; she was a strong little thing. She had weathered a tough storm. I knew she would have more sad days to come, but the worst was over.

I thought of how far I had come too. I reflected over the past three and a half years and identified many changes in me. I did not make a big deal out of things spilling or breaking anymore. Stuff happens, and if it was fixable, it was not worth my time to stress about it. I also stopped beating myself up over everything I did wrong in my life. I accepted that I did the best I could do with what I had at the time.

I live in the present much more now, and I carry a heightened awareness of what can be lost in the blink of an eye. I truly comprehend that I control nothing; I can control only my reaction to it. Understanding this truth brings me profound peace.

I still have grumpy days. I still swear, lose my patience, and continue to think the roads were built just for me. Every day I work to be a better person by beating down my ego that tells me, "You deserve better than this." I don't *deserve* anything. When I mess up, I look up, and I ask God to help me do better next time.

Losing Matt has softened me and allowed me to let others into my life. No longer do I keep up a wall believing that accepting help is a sign of weakness. I know I would not have survived without the love and support of others. I finally get the adage that it's harder to ask for help than to deny it. I'm stronger now, and it's my turn be a resource to others dealing with loss or pain.

I'm closer to my daughter. We always had a great relationship, but it's on a deeper level now, one that we reached through mutual loss. Circumstances have allowed me to be a stay-at-home mother, and I relish the gift of time it allows me to give to her. She does not question if I will be there for her. I am her rock, and she knows it.

If I hear of a death on the news or I happen upon the obituaries in the newspaper, I feel no satisfaction of shared pain. I think of all the people the death must be affecting, and I'm saddened. *Who is getting the tragic news today? Whose world just shattered?* I pray at night for those who are in the misery of hopelessness. I've been there, and it's the worst place I've ever been.

If I were asked, "Would you live your life all over again, knowing you would suffer such a great loss?" I would answer without hesitation, "Yes, I would." As the character Shelby says to her mother in *Steel Magnolias*, "I'd rather have thirty minutes of something wonderful than a lifetime of nothing special." I enjoyed a remarkable, sixteen-year marriage to a great man. Matt Bell asked *me* to marry him. He loved me and cherished me for almost half my life. He made me a better person, both during and following his life. I now know how to love someone without conditions or protective walls.

I no longer think Matt ruined me for all other men. I believe he has prepared me for another great love. Perhaps it's my turn to introduce true love to someone else, to show someone what it's like to be cherished. I trust love will happen with Matt's blessing, maybe even his assistance.

I've seen death's outcome, so I don't fear mine or anyone else's as I once did. The fear of death has been beaten out of me. No person lives one day more or less than God intends.

We all start in this world by being dealt a hand. It includes talents, opportunities, struggles, and obstacles. We also carry with us God. He is in each and every one of us.

Let me share with you the Native American legend of two wolves:

One evening an old Cherokee man told his grandson about a battle that goes on inside all people. He said, "My son, the battle is between two wolves. One is evil. It is anger, envy, jealousy, sorrow, regret, greed, arrogance, self-pity, guilt, resentment, lies, false pride, superiority, and ego. The other wolf is good. It is joy, peace, love, hope, serenity, humility, kindness, benevolence, empathy, generosity, truth, compassion, and faith."

The grandson thought about it for a minute and asked, "Which wolf wins?"

The old Cherokee man simply replied, "The one you feed."

Because of all I've been through, I'm more aware of my actions and mindful of which wolf I feed.

35

Matty

I worked through college at the Midway Motor Lodge, a hotel in Eau Claire, Wisconsin. It contained a restaurant, lounge, and banquet facilities. I was hired to wait tables in the banquet department, and Matt Bell was hired a short time later as a waiter in the restaurant. I won't say it was love at first sight, but we definitely noticed each other. Six months later, Matt asked me out on our first date. From that moment on we were inseparable, and five days following our first date, I told my roommate that he was the man I was going to marry. I knew he was the one for me, and fortunately he felt the same way.

He proposed two years later and we wed on August 3, 1996. The day was absolutely the happiest of my life.

Matt and I continued to work in the area for about three years before Matt told me about Comair Connection Academy, a flight school in Sanford, Florida. He'd always dreamed of being a pilot, and I'd always dreamed of a winter without snow, so in the fall of 1999 we flew down to tour the school. We were both impressed with what we saw, so Matt enrolled. He began classes in January 2000, and I landed a pharmaceutical sales position the same year.

The years following were the best years of our lives. I had a prime job and he realized his goal of becoming a pilot. We took full advantage of his travel benefits and flew all over the world. We loved traveling together, seeing new countries, and experiencing their culture. The time was carefree and idyllic for us.

Our marriage worked well, not only because we were in love with each other, but also because we had a high level of respect for each other. I've always believed that respect was more important than love. People will hurt someone they love more easily than someone they respect.

We were always on the same path, and if one of us wanted to change the course, the other one was willing to get up to speed and follow. You do have to give one hundred percent in your marriage, but you also have to be prepared to give even more to make up for any percentage your partner can't or won't give, if you as a couple are in a rough patch.

We each seemed to hold the pieces that the other was missing. We were each other's greatest champion and gave the other credit for every accomplishment. We pointed out personal shortcomings to each other, to make the other one better. You have to truly love and trust someone to listen to him or her point out your faults without getting defensive.

We knew each other's deepest embarrassments, humiliations, and vulnerabilities. We looked at these things not as flaws, but as areas we could help the other improve. We were truly better together than apart. We didn't start out at such a high level, but our commitment grew as we realized each other's contribution to our own growth and success. We came to value each other's needs as much as our own.

Learning to be grateful was instrumental in keeping our marriage great. I had watched an Oprah episode on gratitude in the early 2000s. The challenge given was that every night before you go to bed, list five things you are grateful for. I talked Matt into doing this exercise with me, knowing we had much to be grateful for. The first few nights it was easy and our answers were obvious and brief; we were thankful for each other, our health, our jobs, our families, and our friends. We seemed to struggle after the first few nights, though, because our answers became repetitive.

Slowly we started to pay better attention during our days, so we had something new to report to each other later. Eventually one reason to be grateful became a short story recited that evening, not a one-word answer. We became more aware of every little thing that happened throughout the day, things we'd never even noticed before. Soon we looked globally and were thankful for all that our country provided to us as citizens. We looked generationally and became grateful for today's technology, medicines, and appliances. I am a little embarrassed to admit that a whole new world opened up for us. *How had we not acknowledged all those blessings before?*

Matt was an exceptional husband. If we were going to drive somewhere, he always picked me up at the door and dropped me off at the door. He couldn't stand the thought of my having to go through an airport alone or having to carry my own bag. After years of marriage, friends would say, "You should see how he lights up when he talks about you," and "You should hear how he raves about you."

He insisted on bringing in all of the groceries, he performed all of the home maintenance, and he took care of our finances, not because I couldn't or refused to do it; he simply wanted to do it. He wanted the house clean and everything taken care of, so that when I got home from work, we could enjoy our time together. I spent a great deal of time in my car driving, as a drug rep, so it got messy quickly, but not when Matt Bell was in town. When I drove into the garage, he'd be out there opening my door, grabbing my workbag, lunch trash, empty water bottles, and coffee mug for me. *Who does that?*

Every January when the presiding president gave his State of the Union address, Matt and I would look at the state of our union. We would use that date as the time for us to come to the table with any gripes or frustrations in our marriage. We'd come clean and honestly state any changes we'd like to see in each other, no grudges allowed. We'd also look over the highs and lows of the previous year and set our goals for the coming year.

He loved being the handyman and doing anything I asked. I'd say, "Hey, Matt, can you sharpen all our knives today?" Done. "Hey, Matt, can you put dimmer switches in the living room and bedrooms?" Done. "Matt, I'd really like to have an outlet right here. Can you make that happen?" Done. "I'd love to have a towel rack in the shower. Do you think you can do that on this ceramic tile?" Done. He could do anything, and if he didn't know how to do it, he'd Google it or ask his friend Steffan.

In March 2006 we welcomed our daughter Ava. We were ridiculously happy and couldn't believe how perfect our lives had become with the addition of our beautiful baby girl. He was a fantastic father. I love that Ava looks so much like him, my Mini-Matt. I love to see his mannerisms come out in her as she grows.

Matt led an impressive life and achieved his every goal, except to become a captain on the 747 and become an astronaut. Given more time, I know he would have reached those goals too. Some things he did and/or got to see in his lifetime included the following:

- He flew the largest jet in the sky; it was a million pounds at takeoff.
- He spent Hawaiian layovers jogging around Diamond Head.
- He ran four marathons.
- He flew over the "bird's nest" during the Chinese hosting of the Olympics.
- He spent a Christmas Eve on the Champs-Elysees in Paris, his favorite city.
- He observed the aurora borealis—the northern lights—at 40,000 feet.
- He saw his favorite band, U2, kick off it's Vertigo concert in Dublin, Ireland, in 2004.
- He sat in the front row at the launch of the space shuttle *Atlantis* in 2010. He was so close that the bleachers where he sat were shaking.
- He fathered a beautiful little girl.

- He cherished his wife and made her a better person, and she reciprocated.

Despite all the amazing things Matt saw in his travels around the world, he also witnessed abject poverty, gender discrimination, and governments that held people in little value. Sometimes the people were bitter and devoid of hope, while in other countries under the same circumstances, people were still happy and thankful for what they had.

He witnessed many things and learned from them, which is why he appreciated his family and friends so much, why he smiled at or talked to people in rough working conditions, why he could no longer accept birthday or Christmas gifts, but instead asked that a charitable donation be made or that he get cash so he could hand it to the first child he saw begging in Asia. He had a true reverence for life and appreciated how fortunate his was.

I remember hearing of Andy Griffith's death in July 2012. The report stated that in the history of television, only three shows have ended while at their peak, *I Love Lucy, Seinfeld, and The Andy Griffith Show*. Matt Bell also left us at his peak; he definitely went out on top.

Was he perfect? Of course not, but he was perfect for me. I miss his big, sleepy eyes in the morning. I miss feeling protected and loved in his embrace. I miss all of his world-travel stories and his hysterical sense of humor. I won't dwell on what I miss, though; I will focus on the joy of today, not on what yesterday took away from me.

36

Children and Loss

I'm hesitant to give too much advice on helping children through a devastating loss. My experience is only with Ava, who was four when her father passed. I've listened to other parents share what their children experienced, but I have not witnessed it.

Grieving in children is as individual as it is for adults, but a huge disadvantage for them is they may not have had little losses along the way to prepare them, if only a little, for the loss of a parent. For children, many things need to be taken into consideration: age, gender, hormonal changes, the number of children in the home, and past experiences.

Children may not have had an opportunity to develop coping skills to assist them with extreme emotions such as rage and depression. They may not have the vocabulary to express their feelings. Friends and family who come to help after a death usually focus on the surviving spouse, because he or she shoulders so much responsibility. It makes sense to get the head of the home back on track first, but please focus on the children too.

Let children express their emotions openly for as long as it takes. Expressing their emotions does not mean they are weak or inferior. It means they have the courage to display painful emotions that make them vulnerable. Not everyone can do it. Encourage them to talk about their feelings and praise them for it. If you enforce silence following a death, you are neglecting your children. You are robbing them of their right and need to grieve. You will cripple them emotionally. If it's too much for you to deal with, get them to a place or person who can help them.

Do not be afraid to cry in front of your children. If ever there is a time that it's warranted, this is it. Do not sweep death under the rug and put a television in front of them. Don't rush to get it over with. I cried more than Ava in the first year, to a point that it annoyed her. She cried more in the second year, free of shame or embarrassment. I'm not an expert on bereavement, and I wish I had done many things better, but in my Things I Did Right column, Allowed Ava to Grieve is one of them.

37

My Advice to Grievers

1. Turn toward God, not away from him.

Only he can walk you through the valley of the shadow of death. Pray for strength and wisdom, and ask others to do the same for you.

You may feel abandoned and forsaken, but your situation is the hand you've been dealt. Believe in yourself because you believe in God. To believe in one is to believe in the other, because he is in all of us. If you put your trust in God, you can overcome anything thrown at you, any trial.

If and when you incriminate yourself for every cross word you've said to the deceased or for every loving word you didn't say, give it to God. Tell him your regrets. Tell him how angry and afraid you are. It takes courage to face the death of a loved one. God will comfort you.

2. Ask for and accept help.

If ever there was a time you needed help, it's now. Needing help does not mean you are weak or incapable, it means you've suffered a great loss. Think of grief as being equivalent to falling off of a building. You've survived, but your body has been pulverized. You need rest, care, and years to recover.

I know you do not want to hear that recovery may take years. You don't want to believe you'll be sad, exhausted, and in pain that long. Remember, the emotions won't be constant, but the road is long. You may think you don't have time for grieving. That sort of thinking is a blaring alarm telling you to slow down and take care of yourself.

You may think that you're tougher than most, so it'll take you less time to recover. Maybe you are and maybe you can handle it better, but you still need help. You need people you can count on when a wave knocks you down.

3. Be grateful.

Remind yourself of all you have to be grateful for, even in the wake of loss. You can always think of something. It will help you see through the blanket of hopelessness that comes with the darkest days. It will take the focus off your loss and put it on your blessings.

4. Honor your grief.

Accept that grief is bigger than you, especially in the beginning. You will go through the stages of grief numerous times, in no particular order. You will feel enormous fatigue, inability to concentrate, anger, and irritability. Your appetite and sleep patterns will change. You will feel guilt, fear, and frustration.

If you try to ignore your grief or bury it, you will only delay the pain. It will fester and resurface at some point, and it will affect every relationship you have and steal joy from your days. Take baby steps to heal. No one is going to applaud if you're "over it" in six months. How long will you grieve? As long as you need to.

5. Cut yourself some slack.

You will wonder when you will feel like yourself again. Feeling better comes in baby steps too. It'll come for an hour and then go away. It'll come for an afternoon and then go away. Eventually it will come for a week and a month. Grief comes and goes for years. Eventually the good days will far outnumber the bad.

Don't hide your pain for fear that doing so will make others uncomfortable or embarrass you. Give yourself permission to let it out, even if you sound like you're crazy. Those who love you will give you a free pass on social etiquette. It's normal to cry a lot.

If you need time alone to just sit in silence, do it. Shut off the phones, television, and radio. Declare yourself off duty. Don't feel guilty if you accomplish little or nothing in the day.

6. Identify who can help you. Stay away from those who can't.

Get help from well-grounded, true friends. Go to family members who have your best interest at heart. If a person has always been kind to you and you know he or she sincerely cares about you, accept that person's help.

Prepare for inappropriate questions. Protect and defend yourself. The questions will come from people either mistakenly or purposely. Either way, look them directly in the eye, pause, and take a breath. If you feel it was an innocent mistake, respond with, "Why do you ask?" Allow them to regroup and correct themselves. If you feel the inquiry was purposely rude, rehearse a response such as, "That's a very private matter and it will remain so."

Make no excuses for staying away from people you know to be ill intentioned. You're in no condition to deal with them on top of your grief.

Don't be angry with people who surprise you by their avoidance. What you've been through scares them, and they are terrified to do or say the wrong thing. These people probably don't have the skills to help you anyway.

7. Believe in yourself.

If you're going through hell, keep going. Force yourself to walk through your pain. Trust that you have the strength and resilience to do it. Focus on today and use the strength you have to get through it. Use tomorrow's strength for tomorrow's problems.

Everyone has something that causes pain in their life, and they must learn how to handle it. The pain can paralyze you or it can motivate you to dig deep and overcome it and come out even better on the other side. Yes, you are hurt, but you're still in the game.

8. Know that the deceased wants you to move on.

Continued grieving does not mean your love was deeper than that of any other's. At some point you need to say good-bye. Accept that the person you lost is gone.

You must revise your life to encompass what it is today and what it will be tomorrow. You must move beyond the way it used to be.

Joyful days will return. Recognize them and savor them when they come. Accept the levity that a good laugh can bring. Laughter does not mean you've forgotten your loss. Laughter and grief can alternate. Allow yourself to come up for air.

38

How You Can Aid a Griever

1. Be there.

If you don't know what to say, say nothing. Just be there. Being there can be tough, because you don't want to show up and stare at the griever. The situation is a no-win. It's very acceptable to say simply, "I'm here for you." Come in small groups if it's easier, and just listen.

Have the courage to call or stop by. At the very least send an e-mail or text message. Don't act as if you're doing the griever a favor by staying away under the guise of, "She'll call me when she's ready. I'll give her some space."

Do not ask inappropriate questions. If a subject was inappropriate before the death, it is even more inappropriate now.

Things I did not want to hear:

"Can you afford that?"

"How are you?"

"Call me if you need anything."

"This could happen to any one of us."

"Christmas must really be hard for you."

"Are you dating?"

"Everything happens for a reason."

"It's been (time frame); you must be better now."

"He's in a better place."

2. Tell grievers that their lost ones knew they were loved.

One of my fears immediately following Matt's death was whether he knew I loved him. Even as great as our relationship was, I questioned it, and I continued to question it for a full year. I was racked with guilt for every fight we'd ever had. Tell the griever, "He knows how much you loved him," and say it again the next time you stop by.

Don't be afraid to say the lost person's name for fear the griever's been struck with amnesia and has forgotten what happened. She is thinking about him every millisecond of every day, and she has not forgotten what happened. Bringing him up will not remind the griever painfully; it will keep his name alive.

3. Try not to cry.

Unless the griever is crying, do not cry in front of him or her. For me, I was barely hanging on, and I had no strength to console others. Step away if you have to cry.

4. Act instead of offer.

Do not say, "Call me if you need anything," or "Is there anything I can do?" Grievers won't call you, and their answer will be "No." Go to their houses and look around. Feed their children, take care of their animals, do some laundry or dishes, make sure the bathrooms have toilet paper, get the mail, go through their refrigerators and clean out rotten food, and throw out dead flowers. If you live in the neighborhood, take their garbage and recycling out to the curb on the designated days.

Bring food reflective of family size. Don't bring trays and pans of food that will rot and need to be thrown away. Here is a better idea: bring a menu from a local restaurant that delivers and include a gift card.

Male friends and neighbors should get together and tell the female griever what day they will be over to perform home maintenance. Look at the lawn, gutters, sprinklers, light bulbs, and so forth. Look at the vehicle tires, oil, and gasoline, anything that a man usually takes care of.

Female friends and neighbors should get together to offer support to grieving men, especially fathers, with tasks that are usually taken care of by women.

5. Help with administrative needs.

Call the utility companies, creditors, and banks. Help the griever update the accounts. Be ready to fax or mail a copy of the death certificate. Don't forget online accounts. No griever wants to get any form of mail addressed to the deceased.

Gather all the documents grievers need and go to the Social Security Administration office with them. Help them claim these benefits and life insurance benefits accurately.

6. Pay attention to the griever's child.

If your child normally plays with the griever's child, keep the playdates going. Take the child to movies, the park, out for pizza, anything. Let grieving children join your family at the beach for an afternoon or have dinner at your house.

7. Don't put a time limit on someone's grief.

Grief is individual. It has no one-size-fits-all length of time. For me, the first year was definitely the hardest, and that situation seems common, but waves of depression still hit me now, three-and-a-half years later. Sometimes when the grief hits, it is as devastating and painful as it was at the beginning.

8. Make every effort to attend the funeral.

It means a great deal to the surviving spouse to see people showing love and respect for the deceased.

9. Let grievers return the favor.

When grievers get back on their feet, let them feel capable. Let them do things for you and give back. I know you did not expect them to return the favors, but let the grievers release their feeling of indebtedness. Helping others helps grievers.

Message from the Author

Thank you for your interest in my memoir.
If experiencing a loss is what brought you to my book,
I am deeply sorry for the loss you have endured. I pray
that my story has benefitted you in some way.

I strongly encourage you to read and follow
http://tealashes.com. Teresa Bruce created this blog,
and it is an exceptional resource offering advice
to grievers and how to help them.